Animal Persuasion

A guide for ethical vegans and animal advocates in managing life's emotional challenges

April Lang, LCSW SEP

© 2016 April Lang, LCSW SEP
This book is dedicated to all the people who tirelessly and passionately devote their lives to making the world a better place for animals. These individuals inspire me every day with their bravery, commitment, and love for all sentient beings.
All rights reserved.

ISBN: 1540617408
ISBN 13: 9781540617408
Library of Congress Control Number: 2016919808
CreateSpace Independent Publishing Platform
North Charleston, South Carolina

Contents

Introduction   v

1	Emotional Onslaught	1
2	Peace, or Piece of Your Mind?	14
3	Romancing the Vegan	23
4	Priming your Progeny	31
5	Fighting the Good Fight	40
6	Serving the Sentient	70
7	Wounded Warriors	97

Conclusion   105
References   107

Introduction

LIVING LIFE AS an ethical vegan can, at times, be challenging. I'm not talking about traveling to remote parts of this country or the world and being unable to find veg-friendly food choices, although that can be frustrating to be sure. I'm speaking about the myriad emotions and relationships we have to grapple with on a daily basis.

Being an ethical vegan means experiencing the world in a way that nonvegans don't always understand. We see beauty and value in all life, not just our mirror images: animals, plants, insects, and our entire ecosystem. Every day, we make a conscious decision to live compassionately. Institutionalized animal abuse is always on our radar. We can't help noticing the countless ways our society marginalizes and abuses animals through factory farming, vivisection, fur farming, entertainment, hunting, and so on. Being conscious of and disturbed by the sights, sounds, and smells of animal cruelty is not something that will ever change. And once we are conscious of this reality, it permeates every fiber of our being.

People who heal, rescue, and advocate for animals have their own set of challenges. Tending to the needs of the world's abused, neglected, and forgotten is often fraught with emotion. How many brutalized animals must one see, hear, or touch before one's dreams are invaded by these images? Sometimes just one.

Seeing the reality of the world is usually a good thing, because we're then better equipped to make more thoughtful choices about how we live our lives. The problem is when what we see, know, and feel overwhelms us to the point that we shut down or shut out. A consequence of this is that our relationships with family members, friends, colleagues, and society at large are often bitter and/or fractured.

So how can we live our lives as ethical vegans and not feel marginalized? Is it possible to attend to the countless animals in need without falling into a dark abyss? How can all of us who care deeply about the plight of animals follow the path that we know to be right and not be overcome by intense emotions? What follows is a guide meant to both assist and support ethical vegans and those that devote their lives to helping animals so that they can not only live but actually prosper in a world that is often harsh and incomprehensible.

Additionally, throughout the book, you'll be reading the personal stories of people who love and respect animals enough to refrain from wearing, eating, and using them as well as the tales of those whose lives are dedicated to aiding and advocating for animals. You'll read about their emotional challenges, bravery, and resiliency. And perhaps these stories will help you with your own struggles as you learn how others have managed to persevere in spite of, or even because of, their challenges. Finally, my hope is that you will obtain some solace in the knowledge that you are not alone in feeling what you feel, thinking what you think, and doing what you do.

1
Emotional Onslaught

There is something about veganism that is not easy, but the difficulty is not inherent in veganism, but in our culture.

—Will Tuttle

HAVE YOU EVER found yourself in one of these situations?

- You're walking down the street on a sunny, crisp autumn day, looking forward to hanging out with your friends, when you become suddenly aware of a lynx, mink, and fox coming toward you, practically obscuring the bodies of the humans underneath.
- Hiking through the woods, communing with nature, your ears suddenly perk up as you hear gunshots ring out in the distance.
- Waiting for the light to change on a busy street corner, you wince as your nose picks up the smell of burning flesh coming from the food vendor half a block away.

- At a summer cookout at your neighbor's house, you're anticipating a delicious veggie burger. One bite, however, and you know it was cooked on the same grill as the "regular" burgers.
- Ten minutes on Facebook reading all the animal-related posts is all it takes for you to begin ruminating on how much, or how little, both you and society have done for the animals.
- Your boss invites you to his house for dinner and afterward ushers you into the den, where you suddenly feel many eyes upon you—the eyes of his hunting "trophies" which encircle the room.

What these experiences have in common is the constant assault on our senses by a world that, for the most part, is disconnected from and disinterested in its use and abuse of animals.

> *I consider myself foremost an ecologically driven vegan because the biosphere is overriding everything in importance. But it seems to have a lesser priority for most people including vegans than personal health and animal rights, and that is hard to deal with. I think that it is due to the natural disconnection and ecological illiteracy of modern humans. Now that I live closer to an environment with more nature, I realize how disconnected I am myself and how little I know. Wish I could communicate this better because time is stacked against us and the vegan solution.*
>
> *My real name is Douglas Dütting, born in the natureless Netherlands and fled to Paraguay, only to realize that the whole world wants to be like Holland.*
> **Douglas Dütting, the Netherlands**

・・・

Now that I am an ethical vegan for the animals and the environment, I feel a hundred times better mentally and physically and healthier. My problem is an overwhelming sadness and anger for the animals, as there are so many people out there who refuse to listen, see, and change. Shopping is horrible, having to pass by the meat and dairy sections. But I keep going forward in hopes that I may be able to change just one person through enlightenment and that my refrigerator is not a morgue and my body not a cemetery and that I am not guilty of speciesism.
Jeannie Hernandez, Queens, New York

• • •

I really want to be a vegan. I know it's the only way to minimize my impact on animals. I'm a lifelong animal lover, which includes companion animals, farm animals, and wildlife. Growing up in the '60s, I was horrified at seeing large sides of beef coming into the local butcher shop. I couldn't understand how others didn't share my distress at seeing bloody animal parts. So it was not hard for me to give up meat in my teens. I frankly never had a real taste for animal flesh and was only able to eat it if it was relatively disguised. Ironically those cows likely led better lives than the billions of animals currently subjected to the horrors of today's factory farming.

So where am I all these years later? I gave up poultry a couple of years ago and am trying to move toward veganism. What I struggle most with is giving up eggs, ice-cream, and pizza. Not to mention I'm responsible for meals for my family of four, two of which are true carnivores driven by the ease and convenience of eating a high protein diet, coupled with a strong belief that carbs and wheat are unhealthy and lead to weight gain.

I've begun the process of researching vegan meal options and in particular vegan baking. I haven't found it easy so far. The first vegan brownies I made were a disaster—could it be that I used prunes instead of dates? But I'm definitely continuing down this path, taking it one meal at a time. However, I wonder if I'm doing enough to put a dent in animal suffering. Is it enough for me to go vegan, or should I be part of the movement to stop factory farming. What do I say when my friends show up in newly purchased coats with fur trim? And will the horror we perpetuate against animals ever end?
Sharon Kessin, Eastchester, New York

These experiences are also likely to trigger profound emotional responses, which can at times be difficult to manage.

Anger is the most common emotional response: sometimes directed at an individual, oftentimes at the world at large. Epithets such as vile, selfish, monsters, and abusers, are often on the tip of our tongues, if not already out of our mouths. Our blood is boiling!

Deep sadness and grief are other emotions that are often experienced when facing an onslaught of deeply disturbing stimuli. Our hearts, our whole bodies, ache for the world's animals. Sometimes the images of suffering invade our dreams and daydreams. Have you ever found yourself engaged in an activity when out of nowhere, you find yourself thinking about animals on factory farms or in research labs? Once we've become aware of the plight of these animals, once we've allowed their suffering to touch us, we may find ourselves consumed with thoughts of their misery.

Feeling frustrated is not uncommon for ethical vegans. We want to do more, but we wonder, what exactly can we do? Ending animal suffering seems like such an insurmountable goal. Where does one even begin?

We had a small local market in our town for many years before they closed. I would routinely do my shopping there because they carried fresh produce, and I prefer to support local businesses. On an average shopping day, I would round a corner, and be confronted with a lobster tank piled with barely moving lobsters, who were crammed in with their claws tied shut. The experience immediately filled me with such overwhelm. I was free to roam the store while these lobsters were waiting in such miserable conditions to die. Although I felt frozen inside, the activity in the store continued as "normal"; the store clerks were stacking the shelves, and the cashier smiled and said, "Have a nice day." I felt such an overwhelming sense of dread, helplessness, and alienation. Couldn't anyone see what I saw? I had fantasies of saying something, rescuing the lobsters, or never shopping there again. How can I be so selfish with my apples and lettuce? Yes, the food in my cart was all vegan, but what about those lobsters? The store finally closed which was a relief, but I've noticed many more stores carrying live lobsters.
H. G., New York

Oftentimes, as vegans, it may seem we're invisible in this world, which can feel both frustrating and invalidating. There are still many regions where our options for food, clothing, products, and so on are severely limited: you find turkey but not Tofurky at the grocer's; ten stores later and still no faux-leather armchairs; cooking shows galore on the Food Network but not for vegans; your vegan option at the town restaurant is iceberg lettuce and a dry microwaved potato. Being vegan is not an anomaly anymore, you hear yourself rationalizing, so choices should abound. Well, truth be told, in many places, knowledge about veganism or even knowing a vegan is still the exception rather than the rule.

My vegan journey began five years ago, after seeing the movie Forks over Knives. Lucky for me, I attended the screening with my best friend, who also adopted a plant-based vegan diet and has been on this wonderful vegan journey with me ever since. Therefore, I was not alone. So much in the vegan world has changed in the last five years. More vegan options at restaurants, more vegan restaurants, and much, much better vegan products (vegan cheese)!

However, I live in New York City, with an abundant amount of vegan choices. I live two blocks from Trader Joe's, around the corner from Whole Foods, the farmers market, within walking distance of several vegan restaurants, and across the street from a vegan sandwich shop. I am so very lucky. I also live in a bubble. NYC is my bubble. A majority of my NYC friends are vegan, so going out to eat with them is not an issue. Most of the events I attend are vegan, so, again, no worries about eating.

Stepping outside of NYC is another story. Traveling thirty miles across the Hudson to NJ, my bubble has burst. I get angry, frustrated, and feel like my hands are tied. How can there be so much progress in the vegan movement, and the plant-based health movement, and be no sign of it just a stone's throw away in the suburbs? Do they not see what I see? Do they not read what I read? Are they not on Facebook!?

I've been at fundraisers for animal shelters serving meat! Seriously? I've been visiting family members in the hospital where nurses were snacking on fried chicken, grilled cheese and bacon sandwiches. The hospital cafeteria's only vegan options were banged up bananas and bruised apples. How can they not have a clue? How can a majority of a hospital staff have adorable pictures of their pets at their stations/desks and still eat other animals???

Dining out with nonvegan friends has been a bit frustrating, but the frustration has not been with my friends supporting me, (as they have—I'm very fortunate to have wonderful lifelong friends). It's been more with them not "getting it." Not understanding that there is no such thing as "humane" meat, and animals are tortured in one way or another for the food, clothing, down comforters, etc. that they buy. They don't want to hear it. They don't want to know where it all comes from and what happens to the animals. I wish I could scream from the rooftops!

So I return to my bubble and do what I can, living by example, spreading the word, and volunteering for events that help the animals.

Lois Eastlund, New York, New York
Designer, Cofounder, LA Fashionista Compassionista Magazine

Then there are times when being invisible, or at least not too obvious about one's veganism, is considered acceptable. *Washington Post* reporter Becky Krystal interviewed two proprietors of vegan restaurants who have chosen not to use the vegan label when describing their restaurants. "He doesn't like the word 'vegan'. He knows it can be an off-putting word to some diners. Often, the perception 'is that we're giving up a whole lot,'" Krystal explained, referring to restaurateur Ran Nussbacher. The second restaurateur, Doron Petersan opined, "I think that while people are becoming more and more open to trying plant-based foods, the vegan label does a disservice" (Krystal, 2016).

So what's the message here for vegans? Essentially, it's that disclosing or highlighting one's veganism publically has risks and should be avoided. While these restaurateurs are doing great work by creating more vegan food options, their misgivings about touting the vegan label feed the public perception that veganism is somehow odd or undesirable, sometimes prompting unwelcome and thoughtless comments. And when we don't feel safe to express ourselves, shame, anger, and sadness are easily elicited.

> *Sometimes I fear being vegan. So many people can become so aggressive against it. I fear posting vegan stuff on Facebook, because I fear how people will react to it. I've gotten so many unfriendly replies that I start to really reconsider my faith in humanity. I get posts like "But it's so tasty!" or "Nobody cares about your cause!" All I've ever wished for people seeing my posts was for them to only just consider the change they can possibly bring about in this world. It breaks my heart every time I see a cruelty video and the lack of compassion in its reaction. I fear that I am still just only one person in still yet a very primitive world.*
>
> *It appears to becoming a fad to hate vegans nowadays. It can be pretty intimidating sometimes. People wonder why there can be such "militant" vegans. I can easily say that it can be quite frustrating dealing with such heartbreaking egocentrism, seemingly called the zeitgeist of the human condition. People may say that animals probably don't have a consciousness. I'd like to ask them: at what point in prehistory did humans magically acquire this consciousness?*
>
> *Living in a society that highly promotes animal agriculture can make me feel like I'm in a morbidly surreal movie, where I find out that humanity isn't as innocent as I once thought. It can be so easy to look the other way and pretend to be in a fantasy world without any cruelty, but I know conscientiously it isn't the right thing to do. It can be so easy to hide amongst the flock in sheep's clothing, but I see all of the corruption in the world, and I know that the world could use a lot of improvement, and I can also thus be a part of that.*
>
> **Jacob, Minnesota**

Feeling demoralized is also quite common. Realizing that trying to get through to people is going to be an uphill battle, requiring the stamina of an athlete, the focus of a yogi, and the patience of a chess master, can be daunting.

> *I am an ethical vegan. I am also an environmental vegan as well as plant-based for health. Even if I was not vegan, I would still be living a plant-based lifestyle. The fear of dropping dead like my father did very young scares me. I inherited a gene from him that causes higher than normal cholesterol levels, and I get it monitored since I am not on medication.*
>
> *It is not an easy lifestyle. However I am committed. I think that by now, my family and friends know that I am serious. I was vegetarian most of my life. I have always been very sensitive to the environment, needs of animals and other people. I have to deal with stupid memes popping up in my feed on Facebook that I know are directed at me and looks from people in the market as they analyze what is in my buggy. My family and workplace have been a big support though. They make sure that there is always something that I can eat.*
>
> *Every day is pain for me. Any time I drive down the road and see a deer in the road, a dog or a cat, my heart aches. Any time I drive by a farm my heart aches. I am a super empath. When I get on Facebook or other social media and see these photos and videos coming through my feed, I cry. I cry every single day.*
>
> *I am a vegan mom raising my son vegan. This met with some challenge from family, who thought that they should be able to go against my wishes. I was very angry with them for a long time. I think they understand now. At least I hope they do. As I stated before, they are very*

supportive. I worry about my son and what will happen when he turns 18. I am hoping that by then the eyes of the world will open more.

Being vegan has driven my social life to a screeching halt. I am a divorced single mom that rescues animals. AND I am vegan. No one wants to put up with that. There are no vegan men in my area—at least ones that are my age. I may just be unattached for the rest of my life. But I am ok with that, because I will do nothing short of practicing what I preach. It sometimes hurts that I am unable to connect with a partner that shares my values.

I find myself biting my tongue a lot. I find no difference between a cow and a dog, and I have gotten into some heated discussions with people because they advocate for dogs and eat cows, etc. I spend my life censoring myself for fear of offending someone. I am to the point now that I do not talk about it unless someone else brings it up. Even so, I get "don't preach at me" thrown in my face even if I am just answering a question. If I want to live in peace, I cannot talk about it at all. My son is forbidden to bring it up around his friends. I don't see anyone who is lactose intolerant being treated that way.

I rescue animals. I run Heart of the Earth Sanctuary and Rescue, Inc. We rescue mostly special needs cats and dogs. They live in a home environment and are family. Our animals are not vegan, as we are a very small establishment and cannot afford to feed them properly with vegan food. We have a dream to evolve into a farm sanctuary, with a program to help homeless people. We take one step forward and two steps back. I live in a farming community in the mountains of Western Maryland. Veganism is not unheard of around here. But to most, people like me are a "freak." Reality is though, the only thing I want to do, my

only goal...is to save animals and help people. Raising money has proven to be a challenge.
Kerry Shoemaker, Cumberland, Maryland, President, Treasurer, & Caretaker, Heart of the Earth Sanctuary and Rescue, Inc.

For some people, these myriad feelings are present at a very young age, when they're just beginning to discover that their connection to animals is on a much deeper level than that of their families. Being different can be especially hard for children, whose views and preferences generally don't carry much weight with their elders.

I looked at the slices of meat my mother handed to me and my brother sitting at the kitchen counter, and I saw the small round white circles in it. I asked what they were and was told they were veins. I knew the white around the slice was fat. I couldn't eat it, and while my brother also said "yuck," he ate his resignedly.

My heart pounding of something being wrong started to take over at this age of ten, all the more disconcerted by the chattering hubbub around me; sitting in a family kitchen and having this plate handed to me by my mother and no one else noticing what was on it.

As I grew up, the feeling I had from a child of lack of recognition coalesced into a triple layer: ignore what's around you; ignore the beliefs of those that care about what's around you; and one step further, celebrate this ignorance.
Emily, Ireland

For others, the family struggle begins later.

It hurts so much to look around and see everything around you for what it really is. Every commercial on TV is a reminder of the torture you have witnessed and the fact that no one seems to care. My transition to veganism included a lot of tears, a lot of guilt, a lot of sadness and emptiness, even loneliness. But I am sooo glad and proud to be vegan and only wish I had done it sooner! For me, the hardest part was seeing people I love, friends and family that I would assume would care as much as me, not seem to care at all. You can tell them all the horror stories, and they say omg that's awful and yet continue to contribute to it. Or they get mad at you instead of mad at the abuse. It's hard. It's hard to hear, "but I can't give up my meat," or "but this is my favorite perfume/makeup," or whatever the thing is, as if that's any justification to continue on with contributing to the torture.

I have had several fights with my family about this. They felt as though I looked down on them because I looked uncomfortable or unhappy every time meat came up or every time they bought products that were tested on animals. At one point I screamed out that they don't love animals—they love their pets—because if they truly loved animals they wouldn't be able to contribute to any of that. This caused a huge fight, and we didn't talk for quite a while. Gladly though, some of my close family seems to be coming around. At least trying to make a small effort with the products they buy. I just wish they'd fully open their eyes already!
Camilla, South Florida

To deal with the flood of feelings, many people often shut down or shut out, and that can take various forms. We might find that happiness eludes us; we don't feel entitled to joyous experiences while animals are suffering, so we turn away from anything pleasurable. The enormity of what needs to be done to change conditions and mind-sets can, for some, be paralyzing. Wanting to take action but being unsure where to begin can engender a state of inertia where people retreat from doing anything, deepening their despair along the way. Distancing or even removing oneself from the sources of one's emotional triggers is not at all uncommon. Invitations to social events go unanswered, family gatherings go unattended, and one's preferred companion becomes oneself. For some who have reached their emotional saturation point, numbing their feelings with drugs, alcohol, or excessive eating is their chosen way of coping. It's easy to become depressed, cynical, and angry about the way our world is and the way our fellow humans act.

> *"It's very difficult to convey which of my experiences, since becoming an ethical vegan (seven years), has been the most deeply affecting. I've seen people perform horrors that I thought were impossible, beneath the depths to which I believed humans were capable, and every day I learn something new, of some new torture device or method in which untold millions of animals are enduring the most heinous suffering and slaughter. If I had to pick one event, it would be the day that I realized that humanity, in general, just doesn't care, doesn't want to know what's happening on an unending basis to the animals they consume, and will fight any attempt by ethical vegans to appeal to their sense of empathy, compassion, or justice. That was the day that I became a recluse. I bought a house in the woods, away from family and friends, and declared my place a vegan sanctuary. I've been called "extreme" and "holier-than-thou" by many people on social media and told I lack "brain protein." I simply cannot understand how advocating for less harm in the world can be considered extreme when the despicable things I see every day are so "mind blowing."*
> **Monica Lucas, Boulder Creek, California**

2
Peace, or Piece of Your Mind?

All truth passes through three stages. First, it is ridiculed. Second, it is violently opposed. Third, it is accepted as being self-evident.

—Arthur Schopenhauer

DOES ANY OF this sound familiar?

- Another holiday dinner with the family and you're all sitting around the table, watching the turkey, leg of lamb, or pork loin being sliced. You grimace, turn away, say something disparaging or perhaps even thoughtful. It doesn't really matter, because regardless of what you say, the response, whether spoken or implied, is usually along the lines of "we don't want to hear it."
- You're watching TV or reading a book when your sister or mom walks into the room, proudly showing off her new Astrakhan coat. You begin to wonder if you were adopted.

- It's college fraternity reunion time, and this year, the vote is for a fishing trip down south. It's at that moment you regret not having chosen the Buddhist fraternity.
- At the office, everyone is once again enthusiastically contributing to a fundraiser for a charity that supports animal testing. "Hmm," you wonder, "this might be the perfect time to see if In Defense of Animals is hiring."

The common denominator here is that you're finding your values pitted against those of the people you engage with regularly and often intimately. There's an internal tug-of-war going on here; one part of you wants to feel close and connected while another part recoils at that thought. And this internal battle brings with it lots of feelings: some expressed, some not.

> Just recently I attended the screening of a documentary called Unity. While it does not focus solely on animal rights, the plight of farmed animals is featured, and I spent a good deal of the film in tears. A few days after watching Unity with one of my closest friends, he and I were texting and he told me that ever since we saw the movie he hadn't been able to eat meat. This was huge, because I cherish this friend, and regardless of what happens in the future, at least on some level someone so important to me finally understood what is in my heart. Just shortly after that exchange, I was speaking to another close friend, someone who has loved me and supported me for two decades. I was sharing with her this revelation, so excited about my other friend's news. Her response? That she wouldn't be seeing any such documentaries with me because there was no way she was ever going to stop eating meat. So, I was reminded of this growing chasm between me and those around me who still consume animal products. And I once again felt that unsettling mix of disappointment,

frustration, and grief, having to acknowledge that when it comes to the importance of animal rights and where people stand on this incredibly pressing topic, there is a line in the sand; and when the people you love are on the other side of that line, it means that your relationships with those people cannot, and will not, ever be the same.
Natalie Forman, Edmonton Alberta, Canada

• • •

For most of my 20s and early 30s, I opened my home to adopted domesticated rescue animals who had been abandoned, often neglected, and essentially disposed of by our anthropocentric society. Some activists have attempted to create names for the widespread cultural conditions that result in speciesism, which is a single word to describe discrimination against animals. There's speciesism, carnism, and I've seen xenophobia applied to animals as well as to various races of humans. But the best term to describe what we have in today's society is human privilege.

"Privilege" is defined as "a special right, advantage, or immunity granted or available only to a particular person or group of people." Almost without exception, those who benefit from privilege are oblivious to it, and never is this more true than when humans look down upon animals as objects rather than seeing them as autonomous individuals with interests, existing separately from each other and from the humans who routinely exploit them.

Around the time of my mother's 60th birthday, I had a guinea pig who was recovering from a major surgical operation. At the birthday party, I told her cousin of the situation, and his reaction was to ask, "Why don't you just get another guinea pig?" The implication was that animals are *replaceable because their inherent value is limited to the value assigned to them by humans, which often is negligible, since humans often assign value to animals based solely on animals' utility to humans. The reason this is possible is because of human privilege. My response to the question was intended to point out the callousness exhibited in this thinking by reversing the situation and putting a human in a comparable situation. My intentionally callous response was to suggest that if one of his human children were to get sick and die, he and his wife could just have another one, since they're all disposable and replaceable.*

Years later, I was talking with the same cousin, who had asked me to explain how domesticated animals are different than wild animals, because he had accused me of exploiting my rescued guinea pigs as pets for companionship. As I was using the term "homeless refugees" to describe these creatures who are totally dependent on humans but are not fully integrated into a human world that unfairly objectifies them, my mother and this cousin burst out laughing. I've never forgiven them for that outburst, and I never will.
Hank P., Walnut, Iowa

Growing up, our family of origin exerts a powerful influence on us, shaping the way we see ourselves and our world, whether consciously or unconsciously. It is through watching their behaviors, learning their values, and understanding their expectations for us that our selves begin to form. While many people accept and adopt the values and traditions espoused by their families, there are plenty of others who end up rejecting them. Our families have a vested interest in hanging onto those traditions because it is through these links to past generations that many families define themselves by. So when we confront our families with our intention to live a vegan lifestyle, they might feel like we're rejecting not only them but all our ancestors as well. Veering away from a prescribed way of seeing and being in the world often requires immense courage because the threat of disapproval, or worse being "cast out" by those closest to us, looms large.

> *Nowadays, I must say I have an extremely supportive family on veganism. The problem was the beginning; the switch was easy for me but hard for others. When I went vegan, I learned the truth must be spoken; with fear and courage simultaneously, I told my mom—she shouted as never before. I remember I wanted to cry, also because I lied I wouldn't be vegan whilst being a secret one (she thought I only dropped meat, but I also did with the other animal products). Veganism was healing me from eating disorders and depression. She didn't even have that reaction when I previously told her I had disorders. It seemed everything was better than veganism, even a past of harm. My family would put animal products hidden in the food they'd try to force me to eat and I refused to; some would provoke laughing and joking about eating animal products and disliked if I didn't see as "jokes"; some made me cry. My mom told this to my therapist, as if it was a disease; I was referred to as an extremist. What I've learned is if I want the support of others, I must first support myself.*
> **Camila Fonseca, São Paulo, SP, Brazil**

The particular community we grow up around also contributes to our view of the world. Like our nuclear families, different cultures and/or subcultures have their own traditions—some quite brutal—which the populace often take pride in. Consider bull fighting in Spain, whaling in Norway, dolphin slaughter in Japan, horse fighting in China and Indonesia, fox hunting in Britain, bear bile farming in China and Vietnam, and rodeos in the United States. When we reject these cultural traditions, we may be perceived as snubbing our own.

Similarly, we are influenced by our peer groups because of the natural inclination to want to fit in. The need to belong, to be accepted, is very powerful. To risk banishment from our social tribe is often as stressful as risking it in one's family.

The manner in which you deal with these varied influences will be determined both by your comfort level in engaging others in potentially hostile discussions as well as the degree of your need for inclusiveness.

Using the scenarios highlighted at the beginning of this chapter, perhaps the simplest approach would be to present alternatives without disclosing your rationale. You could suggest that the centerpiece for the next holiday dinner be a vegetable casserole, take your mom or sister shopping at a vegan clothing store, extol the fun factor of a snorkeling or sailing expedition, and offer up animal-friendly charities for future contributions. All are options that would reflect your values.

You could also vocally express your outrage, disappointment, or sadness to your family, peer group, or community. In this situation, depending on your tone and actions, you will either be given the opportunity to state your case or you might be shut down. Generally speaking, when we're trying to get people to understand our point of view, hurling profanities is unlikely to foster receptiveness. When people feel attacked, they either tune out or fight back, neither response being conducive to changing hearts and minds. This is not to say that you shouldn't be strong and confident in expressing your views; just be mindful of your approach.

> *I work for a major corporation in the automotive industry as an industrial cleaner. One day at lunch, I went to heat up some vegan chili in the cafeteria. One of my co-workers jokingly asked what kind of meat I used in it. I laughed and replied, "Nothing had to die for my lunch today." One of my other co-workers asked if I was a vegetarian, to which I*

> replied, "Vegan, actually." Someone had chuckled and asked, "Isn't that a little extreme?" At first I was mildly offended but then realized that this person is most likely unaware of the damage their lifestyle truly causes. I began explaining to them the horrendous living conditions and unethical practices that take place on factory farms. They had no idea what went on in the dairy industry or how animal agriculture is the leading cause of destruction to our planet. At one point, one of my co-workers jumped into the conversation, agreeing with me and bringing up other valid points to my side of the debate. By the end of lunch I felt as if everyone in that room had learned from what we had to say and were looking at it from a much different point of view. I feel that educating others will help to inspire them to make the connection and choose more ethical and sound choices.
> **Brian Brown, Windsor, Ontario**

Finally, you could withdraw from the people, groups, or situations that you find objectionable. The withdrawal could be a one-time boycott, such as refusing to participate in your neighborhood's annual clambake. Again, you have the option of letting people know why you're not partaking of the "festivities" or just silently bowing out. Your withdrawal could also take the form of a permanent separation, such as changing peer groups or no longer associating with family members. Clearly, the latter option is the most extreme, so think long and hard before you permanently sever ties. If you are certain you have no other recourse, then you must do what is right for you.

> When I first went vegan, my mother was quite condescending about it, making comments like "everything lives at the expense of everything else" and "It's eat or be eaten," accompanied by glum predictions on my future health (such as protein deficiency) if I continued not consuming animal

products. She considered it rude to refuse food that is offered so suggested that I at least not be vegan when I was out and even named other so-called "vegans" who ate animal products when offered them.

When I had children, my mother was enraged that I intended to bring them up as vegans, claiming that I was "ruining their lives" as they would be unhealthy and friendless social outcasts. It was not safe to leave the children alone with her, as it was clear she thought it was her right to feed them animal products. In front of me she would continually offer my children nonvegan food, as if forgetting they were vegan. She would say something like "Would you like an ice cream?" (or Tim Tam or other non-vegan food) and then follow it with "Oh that's right, you can't have that; your mummy won't let you." Needless to say, this put a strain on my relationship with my mother, and in fact we had no contact for some fifteen years.
Anonymous

There is another, albeit less dramatic, approach. Instead of focusing on how unsympathetic or oblivious the people you know are to the plight of animals, you could bring your attention to the good things they have done for you or that they do in their lives. When you needed a down payment for your first house or apartment, your parents happily presented you with a check. There was the year your partner walked out on you, and your siblings were a constant source of emotional support. And after your surgery when you were stuck at home for weeks, your friends pitched in to help you get through that period. When a hurricane hit your town, the community pulled together to provide food, clothing, and shelter to those in need. Then there's your cousin, the volunteer firefighter, and your neighbor who volunteers for Habitat for Humanity. What these examples show is that we're oversimplifying when we categorize people as good or bad. People can still be decent beings even if they're not yet accepting of our views about veganism.

Not everyone's consciousness is ripe for change at the same time or pace, and if we shut these people out of our lives entirely, we may not only be relinquishing the opportunity to open up their minds at a later date, we may end up abandoning some really good people. So while in the short term it may be difficult to accept that those closest to us just don't "get it," that's not to say they never will. And if we can deal with them respectfully and patiently, there's a greater chance they'll at least keep an open mind to our views. But again, each of us has the right to decide what we're willing and able to tolerate.

> *As I continued to see my body's aging time clock roll backwards, my youngest daughter announced she was going vegan. At that point my wife, son, and oldest daughter were staunchly against vegan as unsustainable and too expensive.*
>
> *I run everywhere as a lifestyle and as people they encountered came to learn I was the husband or father of them, the compliments motivated them to reconsider.*
>
> *Over time, I noticed each of them was eating more of a plant-based diet and more fruits. The talk about a vegan diet being unhealthy and unsustainable gave way to announcements that they had not had anything animal in weeks and now months. The mood swings from being under carbs went away.*
>
> *One of the motivators for my wife to go fully vegan was that our youngest daughter went vegan, and once my wife was out to the other two kids (middle son and oldest daughter), they are almost completely vegan now too. My oldest daughter, who has been most adamant that my talk of veganism is foo-foo, recently informed my wife that she is moving towards being vegan. My dreams have come true.*
> **Erskien Lenier, Corona, California**

3
Romancing the Vegan

It takes two to speak the truth: one to speak, and another to hear.

—*Henry David Thoreau*

YOU REALIZE YOU'VE turned onto "the bumpy road to love" when

- your partner informs you that he or she no longer wants to be vegan;
- you tell your partner that you are becoming vegan, and he or she is not supportive of your decision;
- finding the right vegan partner has become your second occupation.

Most people, when they decide to enter into a relationship, do so because they have shared interests, goals, and values. These common elements, along with mutual respect and goodwill, allow the relationship to thrive. If, however, there is a change in any of those elements, it's a signal that it is time to reexamine the partnership. And that is exactly what must happen when one of the partners decides to either opt in for or out of veganism. Living the life of an ethical vegan indicates you have a particular set of values—namely, respect and appreciation for all life—and thus the intention to inflict no harm on any living creature. When one's partner seems to have abdicated those principles or doesn't respect their significant other's decision to live by them, the relationship could be in danger of derailing. Of course some relationships can still survive and prosper in spite of these changes, while in others, the nonvegan partner may eventually open his or her mind and heart to all the benefits of a vegan lifestyle.

In one way, romantic relationships are similar to those we have with our families in that we often feel disappointed or angry when our desire to live as vegans is neither accepted nor respected. One of the primary differences between these two relationships is that with the latter, our choice of blood relations is not an option while with the former, we are free to select a partner whose values mesh with our own. Therefore, when our significant other ceases to feel the way we do about veganism or is not sympathetic to our need to follow that path, it can feel like a betrayal of the relationship. And this kind of betrayal can often kick up an array of uncomfortable feelings.

If your partner is renouncing veganism, the repercussions to the relationship could be substantial. The two of you might have initially bonded over being vegan and/or animal activists. You probably share many vegan friends and frequent a wide variety of vegan restaurants. You may start wondering if you both still share the values that brought you and kept you together. "Does he still believe factory farming is wrong?" "So she thinks eating animals is now OK?" "Has his heart hardened to the terrible conditions endured by so many of the world's animals?" "Will I now have to watch her eat meat at home?" "Can I still love someone who doesn't share this core belief of mine?" What the ramifications of this change might be could begin to weigh heavily on you, bringing up strong emotions in the process, like anger and sadness. You may fear the demise of your relationship.

Now is the time to have an open and honest talk with your partner. If he or she is renouncing veganism, try to find out why. Did a medical professional counsel him to do so for health reasons? Is she getting pressure from her peers or family? Or is it something else? What, if anything, might persuade him to reconsider? If her decision is final and her rationale for giving up on veganism denotes a turning away from veganism's values, then you have to decide if this is a deal breaker for you. Some people might feel that if the relationship is solid enough and there are other shared interests and values, it's worth staying with their partner. For others, this would be cause enough to end things. Do what feels right for you.

If you're the one in the relationship who has decided to become vegan and your partner is not on board, you too may begin to question the viability of your partnership. And as the truth unfolds, don't be surprised if you find yourself feeling hurt and/or disappointed. "Doesn't he want me to be true to my beliefs?" "If she doesn't support me in this, how can I trust she'll be supportive at other times?" "Is he not as kind or compassionate or loving as I had thought?" As in the first scenario, try to find out what his or her objections and fears are. Is she worried about the effect on your social lives—for example, giving up common friends, restaurants, and activities you've both enjoyed? Does he fear being constantly pressured to become vegan and then shamed if he doesn't? Is he or she worried about being abandoned once you adopt veganism? It's important to speak with your partner about his or her concerns, affirming that your shift to veganism won't diminish your love, if, of course, that is the truth.

> *My ten-year marriage ended, in part, because I became vegan and an animal rights activist and my husband didn't. We had our problems beforehand, but this ethical difference between us became a chasm I couldn't tolerate.*
>
> *I tried to make it work. I talked to people in "mixed marriage," where one person is an ethical vegan and the other*

is not, to see what I could learn. I sought out a vegan/AR therapist specifically to address this issue. I read articles. We talked about the impact of this ethical choice on each of us and our relationship in our couples counseling.

Despite all this talking, I realized that given who I am, I could not feel completely safe and connected to him in the way I needed to in an intimate relationship. People like to defend their choices to participate in animal exploitation by saying it is a personal choice or a personal journey to which I now say, "I thought that personal choices were ones where no one gets hurt." To me, whether or not to be involved with someone who does not share the core belief that veganism is a moral baseline is a personal choice.

I don't know whether or not my husband and I could have ended up making each other happy if veganism had not entered our lives. I am sad that it didn't work out, but I am happier than I've ever been in living a life that reflects my authentic self.
Beth Levine, Rockville, Maryland

As you begin contemplating whether to stay or go, do consider the type and length of the relationship as well as its quality, as these factors are likely to influence how much you want to fight for it. Is it a legal arrangement such as a marriage or domestic partnership? Is it a new relationship or a long-standing one? Is it casual or serious? Are there children involved? Has the relationship been a relatively happy one, or has it been dysfunctional for a while? It's best to consider all facets of the partnership before making a hasty decision.

I have been vegan and vegetarian for most of my life, since I was a young teenager. I am now forty-five years old. I have had many relationships throughout that time, with vegans, vegetarians, pescatarians, and carnivores. Without a doubt

my relationships were always smoother and more fulfilling when I dated someone who ate the way I did. From a practical perspective, eating is a huge part of life and a source of connection, and eating in a similar way makes cooking and going out to eat infinitely more enjoyable. Most importantly though, eating in alignment with my values and being in a relationship with someone else who shared my values was an integral component for me to deepen my connection with them. I dated a die-hard meat eater for ten years. We never cooked a meal together and rarely ate together. Going out to dinner always left one of us compromising. While I loved him and we tried to make it work, we eventually parted ways—for many, many reasons, not just food choices and ethics around animal protection. I ended up marrying a fellow vegan, and it is lovely to cook and eat together and to be mutually excited about trying vegan foods and restaurants. Over the years I have learned that having a partner who eats and lives in alignment with my values is fundamental for me. I am very committed to animal protection, and if I ever do find myself being single again for some reason, I am clear that vegan eating is a must in any future potential partner.
Kimberly, New York, New York

If you have decided to stay with your nonvegan partner, it would be advisable to clarify the expectations you have for each other so there are no misunderstandings about how you'll be handling this aspect of your relationship. Will there be separate shelves or pots or utensils for storage and cooking of nonvegan foods? Will your partner concede to eating vegan at home? Will you acquiesce to eating at nonvegan restaurants? If your partner chooses to engage in animal-centric activities or conversations that are anathema to you, how will you respond? Expect ongoing negotiations if the relationship is to thrive.

For those that have been fortunate to have a partner willingly embrace veganism, there is cause to celebrate. Seeing firsthand the transformation of someone you love into an even more evolved and compassionate person is quite powerful. And together, you have the potential to make great things happen in the world.

> *I've been with my girlfriend since 1994. She was almost vegetarian when we got together. She immediately became full on vegan without hesitation. It meant a lot to me that she was willing. It made our bond stronger. I think it can be difficult if one person is vegan and the other isn't. It can lead to questioning each other's choices, putting strain on a relationship. Coexisting with someone who eats what you do is a lot easier obviously than being with someone who doesn't, but it's not impossible. It's so helpful to be with someone who has a similar belief. Being vegan is a matter of faith. I don't want to push it on people. You have to know it's the right thing to do and still one of the most powerful actions one can take to make life better on earth. In 2005, my girlfriend and I created a food business making veggie food at music festivals. It's lucrative and is a form of nondenominational missionary work of sorts. We have opened many, many carnivorous mouths and minds on our journey. It feels great!*
> **Anonymous**

"Oh where, oh where, can my vegan mate be?" is not an uncommon lament among ethical vegans. Of course there are some dating sites for vegans, vegetarians, and eco-conscious people, but the reality is that the numbers pale in comparison to the more mainstream sites that cater to a broader clientele. And while there are many more ethical vegans around these days, there's clearly not enough to swell the dating sites. So while it's not impossible to find an ethical vegan on

Match, eHarmony, Grindr, or Tinder, just don't expect a huge pool of prospects, especially in less populated areas. The road to true love can be bumpy indeed. As more people begin to adopt the vegan philosophy and lifestyle, one's choices will undoubtedly increase. But in the meantime, you may wonder if there is any pool of prospects from which to choose. Of course there is. You can contact all your vegan friends and ask them to introduce you to all their potentially eligible pals or throw a party where each friend you invite must bring along a guest who is a single vegan. Instead of perusing dating sites, join Meetup groups or activity clubs which were created for vegans or vegetarians. For instance, check out groups interested in vegan cooking, restaurant hopping, or animal activism. You may even find some like-minded people in groups which don't have an explicit vegan agenda but which share the philosophy of do no harm or have an appreciation for nature. Consider looking into groups whose focus is photographing wildlife, visiting nature preserves, biking through scenic landscapes, or starting gardens, assuming of course that these activities interest you. Or be a leader and start your own group. You never know who will pop in. These are just a few ideas, but see how creative you can be in coming up with others. Of course if you do meet a terrific person along the way who is not vegan but is openhearted and open-minded, you just might influence them to adopt a vegan lifestyle. But don't bet your future on this happening. Getting into a relationship with the hope or expectation a person will change is a very bad idea. If it happens, great, but there are no guarantees. So before you contact that cute guy or gal or accept their offer of a date, decide what your parameters for dating will be. Are you willing to date nonvegans? What about vegetarians who may or may not turn into vegans? And of course, even if you begin dating an ethical vegan, that alone is not enough to ensure you'll live happily ever after. It takes more than a shared commitment to ethical veganism to create a happy, fulfilling, and lasting relationship.

Being an ethical vegan and dating…Sucks.

People who don't get it, don't get it…and I have a debate with myself as a single person doing online dating if I should list vegan in my profile. On one hand maybe there is a vegan out there searching for another and on the other hand…I know many people fear the V word and will immediately label me extremist and therefore limit my dating options. One of my tests is when men list themselves as animal lovers—I ask them how long they have been vegan. That is a good way to weed them out. I used to feel like someone needs to meet me before I came out, see that I'm cool and sexy and "normal," without a preconceived idea of me being an "annoying" extremist vegan. Now, I tell them pretty early on. It definitely shows the level of interest a man has…whether or not he is considerate in choosing restaurants.

And for those who aren't, there is the dilemma of going to dinner—what if he eats meat and I kiss him and taste it? I broke it off with someone because he tasted like steak. It was a total turnoff, and I couldn't bring myself to kiss him again.

A few years ago, I met a woman, an attorney and animal rights/veganism advocate, who had just gotten married. I asked how she found such a hot vegan man—because I have not met that many. Her words were wise: "You have to make your own."

When I think about a long-term partner—could I be with someone who wasn't vegan, be in a home with meat and leather—the answer is…I don't know. And this is a huge dilemma. Huge. When I meet men I like—one of the big turn ons is when I sense that they have "compassion possibility"—potential for conversion—so I too can make my own.

Aimee, New York

4
Priming your Progeny

To bring up a child in the way he should go, travel that way yourself once in a while.

—Josh Billings

WELCOME LITTLE BABY,
   It's almost time to eat.
   Now here's your first lesson,
   There won't be any meat.
   As you lovingly gaze into the eyes of your new next of kin, you realize that you just brought another life into this world that will share your resolve to live a cruelty-free life. And you vow to do everything possible to make that a reality. You'll take your child to animal sanctuaries. You'll explain why taking another's life for one's own pleasure is wrong. You'll cook delicious vegan meals. You'll do your darnedest to ensure your child doesn't equate veganism with deprivation. You start off confident that it won't be difficult to mold this child into seeing the world as you do. But that confidence begins to wane after getting a whole lot of pushback from others, including your child:

- Meat smells so good!
- Everyone's making fun of me because I don't eat meat.
- Can't I have just a bite of the Big Mac?
- All the kids were sharing their lunches, but nobody wanted mine.
- Do I have to be vegan when I grow up?
- You're going to make her sick with this vegan nonsense.
- I can tell you now, when he comes to my house I'm feeding him normal food.
- One hot dog isn't going to kill her.
- What kind of doctor thinks this is OK?

There are many moments when our lifestyle is at odds with the mainstream, and at times our children take notice and ask questions. We'll occasionally visit local farms, most of which grow plants but also raise animals. On our latest visit, our girls asked whether this one was "a good farm," meaning, are they nice to the animals. The farm is a beautiful place, idyllic looking, where they seem to treat the animals with lots of care and respect. Still they will be slaughtered. So what's the answer then? Everyone there was enjoying themselves—the farmworkers, the other visitors, and us too as we walked around admiring the plants and animals. Even the animals, eating, playing, sleeping, somehow seemed content. And I almost felt guilty as I lay the confusing truth on my children about the ultimate purpose of the creatures on that farm.

The discrepancies aren't just what we witness around us. Our kids have internal struggles too with their occasional desire to eat animal-based foods. Outside the house, from time to time, we'll let them eat a small amount of dairy or a few bites of a hot dog at a party. Our younger daughter seems to reflect on this more than her sister does. She'll talk about

wanting to still be vegan or vegetarian when she grows up, but that she does sometimes like to eat turkey for example, which she did at school this past fall during a Thanksgiving celebration. Yet the week before, in that same classroom, she was quite upset by a poem the class learned which tells of a turkey running away from a farmer. She was so upset, in fact, that the teacher modified the class activity with the poem. Despite her choice to eat a slice of turkey next to her classmates, I think there are enough times at her young age (now six) that she makes the intellectual connection between the living animals and the food on people's plates, and I hope that as she and our older daughter grow up, their choices will be consistent with their values.
Elizabeth van der Zandt, Dobbs Ferry, New York

You're now deflated and possibly a little concerned. Your dream of adding a new vegan to the world now seem a little less certain as you begin to grapple with some difficult questions. "Will I ever be able to exert any influence over my son? Am I causing my daughter emotional distress? How strict should I be? What if my child sees my disappointment? Will raising my child as a vegan cause a rift in my relationship with family or friends? What'll be my strategy when others try to undermine my efforts?" These are all reasonable questions and concerns, so let's look at a few facts.

You can teach your son or daughter all the reasons being vegan is important and model a happy and healthy lifestyle, but there's no guarantee any of this will resonate with your child. Think of it this way. You may adore piano and hope to instill this same passion in your child but find that your kid would rather hit a soccer ball than a piano key. And what about the child that grows up to be an atheist after being raised by religious parents? Reflect back on your own life for a minute. Did you follow all of your parent's recommendations for living a successful life? Probably not. However, that didn't necessarily mean you didn't value their opinion or that you never accepted their counsel. So just because your child doesn't respond to veganism the way you hoped he or she would, do not presume your child will never heed anything you say. When we have children, it's normal to want to guide them toward living the kind of lives we believe are right and best for both them and the world. And it's certainly not a foregone conclusion that your child will go left when you say go right. But it is possible, and that possibility is important to keep in mind—both before you have kids and while raising them. So be mindful of the expectations you have for your child, and keep them in check; unspoken and unmet expectations can lead to disappointment and damaged relationships.

> *I was reading a book to my nine-year-old daughter where the main character is a pig. Her mother was serving her bacon for breakfast, which would make her a cannibal. Pigs do not eat other pigs. This is an example of the constant struggle for vegan parents to raise vegan or vegetarian children. It's a much larger landscape than consuming animals for food. It's about ethical choices that we want to impart to our children without pressuring them, scaring them with stories of atrocity, or strongly influencing them with our own beliefs. A child's world is constructed of constant anthropomorphizing of animals. For example, almost every book we read has "happy" animals, including farm animal characters. This conditioning leads our children to a collective numbness to all nonhuman animals and to their plight. Our children witness most of their friends and family members consuming animals for food, wearing animals for clothes and shoes without any knowledge of their suffering.*
>
> *So what do we do as a family? We educate our daughter though our actions, and we model compassion toward all. We are sensitive when we explain our reasons for why*

we don't eat, wear, use, or even visit animals in cages. We treat our beloved cats and dogs with dignity and respect and let her know that all animals deserve the same respect. We don't kill bugs in our home (our daughter has become quite good at taking them outside herself). We teach her respect for all life. We answer her questions as honestly and openly as we can. We try to visit and experience animals in their natural habitat (such as farm animals) as much as possible so she experiences a more alive connection to them. Perhaps, the most difficult of all is we let her make her own choices. So far, she is not interested in eating animals. However, one day she may, and we will need to come to terms with this reality. Regardless, we believe that she will be forever compassionate, caring, and kind toward all beings.
Heidi L.G., New York

If your child comes to you expressing reservations about being vegan, really try to hear him out without judgment. A child that feels heard and not judged is much more likely to approach you when something is bothering her, vegan related or not, than a child who fears that expressing her opinion will anger or disappoint you. And never shame your child for having a different viewpoint than you or for questioning your values. It would be like your family shaming you for choosing veganism. When we grow up feeling ashamed of our feelings or opinions, we may start to doubt their validity, our right to have them, or even our self-worth. Ultimately, we may stop expressing ourselves entirely and end up frustrated, bitter, and depressed. Also keep in mind that many tweens and teens are eager to fit in with their peers. So don't be surprised if this is the time when your child has a mini-revolt against veganism.

While it's important to always be clear with your child (in an age-appropriate way) about why you believe being vegan is important and be willing to address the subject when he or she brings it up, it's best to avoid constant proselytizing. Otherwise, you might end up with a child who rejects veganism solely to forge an identity separate from you and/or the family—or just to be contrary, as kids can often be.

> *When my husband faced some health challenges four years ago, we transitioned to a whole-food, plant-based diet. Since we, as parents, have been finding our way on this path, we've found that our reasons for eating a vegan diet and extending that into other areas of consumption (clothing, furniture, etc.) have expanded greatly beyond our personal health. I try to communicate clearly with our kids about the reasons for our choices, even as those reasons evolve. The fact that they're young sometimes makes it difficult; I don't want to present gruesome stories or details, yet I want to impress upon them the harm that some choices can cause. Our daughters were one and four years old when we eliminated animal foods, so our older daughter already had a taste for them. Still, our kids are quite happy to eat the foods we do at home. The challenging moments come in social situations: birthday parties, school celebrations, holiday parties with friends. Macaroni and cheese, the hot dog at a neighbor's barbeque, scrambled eggs at a friend's house…any of these can be a challenge. When every other child at the table is eating pizza—and their parents are happy to serve them—it's hard for a five year old to rationally make the healthier, less harmful choice or as a parent, to force her to do so.*
> **Elizabeth van der Zandt, Dobbs Ferry, New York**

As a vegan parent, you have every right to set the standard for what your child will eat at home. But depending on how adamantly your child resists being vegan outside the home, you may decide you need to compromise a bit. But don't forget that kids change their minds often: at five, your child was going to be a doctor; at ten, the president of the United States; at sixteen, definitely a lawyer; and at twenty-one, no clue! So even if your kid isn't gung ho about being vegan now, the principles you worked hard to instill in him or her might take root in adulthood, and veganism it will be. But if that doesn't happen, think long and hard about the stance you will take and the attitude you will adopt, as both have the potential to influence your relationship with your son or daughter. Expressing disappointment in a decision is fine; making your child feel he or she is a disappointment to you is not fine.

Because we live in a world where veganism is not universally understood, valued, or accepted, don't be surprised if those around you, including family and friends, pipe in with their opinions and warnings about the dire consequences of raising a vegan child. While everyone is entitled to their opinions, they don't have the right to lambast you for making different choices. While you should always feel confident in your enlightened decision to raise your children according to the principles of Ahimsa, it would be prudent to give some thought to how you might respond to potential naysayers before you have children, as well as what behaviors you will tolerate and from whom.

> *The hardest part of raising a vegan child is definitely a pressure that I get from my family and from some of my friends. Most people are still concerned about not getting enough nutrition if you don't eat meat, especially protein. I always calmly explain vegan is not a veggie diet, and I am not forcing my crazy diet to my son. It's a lifestyle that avoids unnecessary pain that animals have to go through. Also telling them other reasons such as environment and health help to explain what vegan is all about.*
> **Hikari Rodriguez, Astoria, New York**

There will likely come a time when your vegan child will face the harsh reality that most of the people in the world don't view and treat animals with the respect and compassion your family does. As it's neither possible nor wise to keep this truth from him, and unless all her friends' families are vegan (which is unlikely), your kid will probably see the sanctioning of hunting, fishing, animal wearing, animal eating, and so forth on a fairly consistent basis. This disconnect between what you're teaching your child and what is tolerated by others might be confusing and upsetting to your son or daughter. The knowledge that animals are routinely abused and killed to benefit the perceived needs and pleasures of people is a truth that must be told, but how and when is something that must be carefully thought out. Consider the child's age and temperament when deciding how to approach this subject, and be as patient and nurturing as possible as your child attempts to make sense of the nonsensical. You don't want this "bursting of the bubble" to overwhelm your kid.

> *I was sitting in the back seat of my brother's car with my five-year-old niece. She was talking about fish and the different colors they are. I mentioned rivers and people fishing and catching them. She jumped forward, her voice upset. "What do you mean? Why do they do that? They must stop. They must put them back in the river and let them be. I'll tell my dad, and he'll make them stop." I explained that some people ate them. She said, "No, the fish in the shop aren't these ones. The fish my mom buys are different. They're okay, nobody has hurt them." I had to pretend that these fish were in fact "different"; they weren't fish that had once been alive.*
>
> *As a child I didn't have the voice to ask these questions; I internalized and stopped eating animals. Which was better? She was asking these questions, but I couldn't answer them truthfully. It was as if meat and fish were Santa Claus, and I couldn't break the myth for her—only her parents could do that. Would she ask these questions again or move through this time of openness in her life and remain in the false*

childhood belief that most adults carry that somehow the fish in the river or the cow in the field magically appear on your plate while still remaining in the river and in the field?
Emily, Ireland

5
Fighting the Good Fight

There may be times when we are powerless to prevent injustice, but there must never be a time when we fail to protest.

—Elie Wiesel

WHEN WAS THE last time you heard or thought these things?

- They're nothing but armchair activists.
- You're a vegan and don't do ANY outreach?
- There's so much to be done; I just don't know where to start.
- Should I focus on one area of animal cruelty or fight them all?
- I can't fix this.
- The abolitionists don't understand that a bit of compromise is necessary if we're going to help the animals who are now living on factory farms.
- The welfarists are in cahoots with the perpetrators! There can be no compromise!
- Am I doing enough?

Accompanying these thoughts are often an array of feelings that being an animal activist can engender: uncertainty or guilt about what and how much you're doing; frustration, anger, or sadness at not being able to affect the change you want, in the manner you deem most expedient; or shame that you're not living up to your or someone else's standards. Whether a professional activist working for an animal welfare/rights organization or an individual working solo to help animals, encountering a diverse group of mind-sets is to be expected. Of course everyone has the same overarching goal, which is to help animals, but often that is where the consensus ends. Each advocacy group has its own philosophies, priorities, and strategies for improving the lives of animals. Similarly, every person is going to have his or her own ideas and capacities for change.

> *I don't work on or have a job as "animal rescuer." I donate $, I go to protests like Sea World, etc., & talk to as many people as I can that will listen. I am (one of many)—a voice for the voiceless.*
>
> *This was the start of my vegan journey, although it would take many years for me to work it out. When I was about ten years old, I was taken by some friends to a slaughterhouse. We went there a few times to watch the process. It was about 1958, & things were different then. I can't explain what I was thinking about at that age. I think I thought that's the way things were meant to be; everything & everyone had their place in life. I ate meat then, & that's where it came from. Now, I look back, & it makes me sad that I accepted "that's the way it was meant to be."*
>
> *I think that all vegans do not understand: "why can't the rest of the world see what we see?" For many years, I tried to avoid places & functions that served meat. I do go to those places now, & I use any opportunity to talk to grocery store or restaurant employees about a healthier & kinder way to*

eat. Frustration & anger is a part of this lifestyle. On the bright side, I have converted at least seven people.

There are those moments when I do feel beaten down & wonder what can I do to change the way people look at & treat all animals? We are fortunate to have organizations like Mercy For Animals, PETA, Vegan Publishers & Last Chance for Animals, etc. We are lucky to have the great documentaries like Cowspiracy, Earthlings, Forks over Knives, Fat, Sick & Nearly Dead, *& more. Words cannot describe their contributions. Thank you.*
Tony Santone, Laguna Beach, California

Deciding what your contribution will be is a personal decision, and no one has the right to tell you you're not doing enough or that what you're doing isn't significant enough. There are many different ways to make a positive impact on the lives of animals, each dependent only on one's inclinations and skills. And while there will be times when you wish you could be doing more or you realize you can't change a particular situation, you mustn't be too hard on yourself. Occasional defeats don't nullify all the good work you've done and will continue to do.

Nerves of steel would definitely describe the people who engage in the most "extreme" activism. By extreme, I'm not implying a value judgment but rather the risk factor. Consider the activists who work undercover at factory farms and slaughterhouses to record the daily abuses of the farm animals. If exposed, they might get arrested or physically harmed, but that doesn't deter them because the alternative for the animals is far worse. There is no question that these people are incredibly brave souls who are doing vital work. But the truth is, not everyone has the disposition to engage in this form of activism. And that's OK because animal activism is "an equal opportunity employer," accommodating a variety of constitutions and aptitudes. The key is being honest with yourself about what yours are. Because once you find what feels right for you, you're much more likely to keep doing it.

What follows are a few examples of ways to channel your temperament or skills for animal activism. These suggestions are applicable whether you go it alone as a freelancer or get yourself hired at an animal organization.

- A good writer? Start writing letters to newspapers, blogs, corporations, and policy makers about an issue(s) you want to publicize or a situation you want to change: local or global.
- Always been the social type? Consider attending or organizing demonstrations or do some tabling for animal organizations.
- Introverted, a political junkie, and prefer using your phone? Contact an animal advocacy organization or your state chapter of the League of Humane Voters to find out which bills and politicians require attention. Start dialing.
- Can't resist touching every animal you see? Don't like being behind a desk or on a phone? Offer your time to an animal shelter or sanctuary or become a wildlife rehabilitator.
- A whiz with the computer? Tech savvy? Pick your favorite animal organization and offer to design, improve, or manage their website or blog.
- Enjoy a good debate? Have a knack for teaching or communicating? Stage fright not in your genes? Consider humane education.
- The entrepreneurial type? Start a petition. Organize a meatless day/week/month at your school, community center, or workplace. What about organizing your own animal rescue/advocacy group?
- No problem asking people to contribute to a cause? You like to follow the money? Perhaps you're a born fundraiser.

- Your camera is practically glued to your hand? Maybe a local animal shelter could use your expertise and passion to take pictures of animals up for adoption.
- Never met a party you didn't like? How about organizing fundraising events for your favorite animal group(s)?
- A private person, not a joiner, and don't feel comfortable calling attention to your lifestyle choices? Then enjoy being who you are, and know that even if you don't lift a finger, you're still making a huge difference for animals by deciding to live as an ethical vegan.

People are drawn to animal advocacy for an array of reasons, not least of which is having witnessed firsthand animal cruelty or neglect.

> *As a child, I connected with films such as* Charlotte's Web *and novels like* Silver Fox—*about a boy who tried to rescue a fox from a steel-jaw trap. Stories of Greenpeace activists who defended whales from killers in giant metal ships captivated me no less. All of these stories helped to confirm my beliefs that nonhuman animals had feelings, their lives mattered, and I should do something to help them. By age ten I decided to become a veterinarian.*
>
> *Seven years later I enrolled in the preveterinary program at New Mexico State University as a Crimson Scholar (an academic status given to freshman with high test scores). The first class of my first semester was Animal Science. Profit from flesh would have been more accurate. The class covered only animals used for food, and it taught such non-science as the marketable pieces of their bodies and the profit rationale behind giving them antibiotics and hormones. Their health mattered only when it affected profit.*
>
> *Animal Science included field instruction where students would interact with nonhuman animals and removed*

parts of their bodies. One day, the teacher brought the uterus of a slaughtered cow and opened it to reveal a dead calf about the size of a football. The class's lesson was how the placenta connected to the uterine wall. All I thought was, "Couldn't they have waited for the calf to be born?" Another day, students chased a ram into a special metal cage that grabbed him and rotated him onto his side. The teacher instructed the students to insert a metal device called an anal electroejaculator into the ram's rectum to force an ejaculation for sperm analysis. As I witnessed this, I thought, "This is rape."

Although I still ate animals, the class shocked me so deeply that I asked the teacher if I could present to the class why some people choose to become vegetarian. He refused.

Today, I doubt that other students would have been receptive. They were all from animal farms where it was normal for their animal friends to be turned into meat. I was from the suburbs. I had never raised a cow, pig, or chicken, nor did human adults convince me that their lives didn't matter. It was not normal for me to turn my friends into meat because I never befriended cows, pigs, or chickens. While Animal Science continued the same lessons that other students learned on the farm, the class altered my worldview. Even though I ate some animals, I previously regarded all nonhuman animals as people with a different anatomy. College forced me to face my inconsistency, why some animals were "friends" and others were "food."

Nor did I previously understand how meaningless the lives of nonhuman animals were to those students who wanted to become their doctors. Animals were just numbers to them—head of cattle or dollars at auction. I could not fathom similar regard to human patients at the hands of medical students. I wanted to become a vet to learn how to make nonhuman animals healthy, but all I was being taught was how to make them healthy enough for slaughter.

NMSU was teaching me to kill people. My morale plummeted. I refused to take the final exam and consequently failed the class. All of my grades suffered, and my academic status downgraded to probation. My depleted morale did not replenish, and I dropped out of college years later.

Animal Science backfired with me. I became vegan soon after leaving college, and it turned my grief into advocacy and activism. My greatest regret is not facing my inconsistency when I was younger.

Jerold D. Friedman, Houston, Texas
Social justice attorney who practices federal law, is an international speaker and author on legal, scientific, and political aspects of vegan and nonhuman animal advocacy

• • •

My name is David Sefelorlor Nyoagbe. I am an Animal Activist and a Humane Educator. I am the cofounder of Ghana Society for the Protection and Care of Animals. I must say before you can work for Animals, you must have a big heart—full of compassion. In this part of the world where I live and work, animal issues do not really matter to a lot of people. Someone once told me, "When there are a lot of human issues to think about, why am I thinking about Animals?" They think human issues need more attention than Animals. I grew up in a culture where children chase animals and throw stones or anything they can find at them, beating them and all sorts of things; hence animals are no longer man's friend.

I became sad and frustrated and decided to speak for the voiceless. At twenty- two, I started a small group called the Friends Club, where we speak on behalf of Animals. We speak to children and Animal owners to treat Animals with love. In the cause of working for Animals, you may feel sad and frustrated at times, but you need to stand up strong and fight their cause because you are speaking for people who cannot speak. You may be sad when an Animal you are helping dies or a situation becomes worse off.

Frustrated when you put in more efforts to educate people to treat Animals with love and care, and they would rather abuse them. Sometimes I get beaten down when people who are supposed to know better would rather abuse and neglect Animals. So-called people who say they love Animals leave their Dogs and Cats without food and clean water for days.

My major hurdle now is how to get people all over the world to know that Animals matter a lot in our lives. When we all begin to change our attitudes towards Animals and treat them with the love and care they need, this world will be a nice and safe paradise to live in, without Animal disease. Safe and clean environments with healthy Animals being treated well equals Animals becoming man's best friend again.

My working with Animals has changed me over the years and given me a lot of compassion and inner satisfaction. Can you imagine what I went through when a public transport on which I was travelling knocked and killed two dogs before the end of a four-hour journey? Man and Animal were created by God to coexist on planet earth. Why should one be abused and neglected by the other? We need to be each other's keepers.

> *Lives of Animals are just like humans. They also have needs. If we want to keep Animals then we must learn to become responsible Animal owners and lovers.*
> **David Nyoagbe, Accra, Ghana**
> **Cofounder Ghana Society for the Protection and Care of Animals**

And for some, having experienced their own physical/emotional abuse or neglect was what motivated them to become animal activists.

> *I could say that for me, the animal cause is like a beloved fourth child.*
>
> *I could tell you that I don't allow myself to think about the animals' suffering because if I did, I couldn't continue my fight for them. The thought of their suffering is a pain too great to bear and would incapacitate me.*
>
> *Both of the above are true.*
>
> *But perhaps, at a level that is uncomfortable to contemplate to any degree, my dedication to the animal cause is for a child deep in the past who wanted to be good enough to be loved.*
>
> *I think many people in the animal cause experienced emotional and/or physical and/or sexual abuse as children, and fighting for justice for those for whom there is none, giving voice to those whose voices the world chooses not to hear, speaking out for suffering that the world does not care about is in fact all for a child of long ago.*
>
> *Yet there is gratitude too for the circumstances of that child because those circumstances created a powerful "calling."*
> **Louise van der Merwe, Cape Town, South Africa**
> **Managing Trustee, The Humane Education Trust**

In order to enact change for animals, advocates need to get the cooperation of other people. For that to happen, it's important to understand how people think and what will motivate them.

> *The first time I was half meter away from a real tiger is in the third week after I joined Animals Asia Foundation in 2010. I was in a meeting with the vice president of a theme park which runs an animal circus on-site. To prove that "the performing animals are absolutely fine," the vice president took me and my colleague to the den of performing animals. I saw the tigers, lions, bears and macaques lying on the concrete floor in dark and wet caves without any food, water, and substrates whatsoever. However, what strikes me more is the confidence on the VP's face—he did truly believe that the "animals are absolutely fine." I have seen many similarly confident faces in the following six years, but this meeting has helped me to realize that it is humans that I am going to concentrate on, as they are the only chance to make a difference for the animals.*
>
> *In the past six years, I have visited dozens of Chinese zoos and safari parks and have seen hundreds of (if not thousands of) animals living in horrendous conditions. When I approach these facilities and talk to people to improve the animal welfare levels, I am still shocked by how "confident" people are when they take care of animals in an inappropriate way and how reluctant they are to make a change. That said, since the first day I started, I am fully aware that animal welfare is a new concept in China and the only thing I can do is to be patient. Therefore, I am witnessing the small progress of my work, and I accept that it will be a slow and long process.*
>
> *I used to think human beings are superior to any other animals. However, the more I read about animal cognition,*

the more I believe we are not superior at all. When I review the history of animal welfare development in the UK and Europe, I believe the lack of understanding animals is the major cause of people's confidence with their poor practices. This job encourages me to think more about how human beings interact with our environment and treat animals, ultimately how we look at ourselves in this world.
Lisa Qing Yang, Chengdu, China
Animal Welfare Dept. Manager, Animals Asia Foundation

• • •

From farming tigers and bears for the trade of their parts to killing dogs and cats in the name of rabies prevention, the human behaviors that inflicted so much pain, suffering, and loss of life are rooted in greed and ignorance. Recognizing the motivating factors of these behaviors is the key in keeping me positive, transitioning from feeling sad to strategies that can remedy the situation.

I used to wonder why my countrymen, Chinese, are prejudiced against elephants, as their desire for ivory as "white gold" incentivized poaching, and resulted in the death of hundreds of thousands of elephants in Africa. I was very glad to have my assumption proved wrong by a survey which found seventy percent of the Chinese did not know ivory comes from dead elephants. In Chinese, ivory is literally "elephant teeth." People don't die from fallen teeth, nor could elephants most people wrongly assumed. It was an epiphany for me. Chinese are not prejudiced against elephants; they are just not informed!

To debunk the myth about the origin of ivory, we developed the "Mom, I have teeth" campaign. Through the voice of a baby elephant excitingly declaring his newly emerged teeth and the subdued reaction of his mother, the ad alludes to the devastating consequences of ivory trade and urges consumers to reject ivory.

The campaign resonated with the Chinese so much so that advertising agencies provided us in-kind spaces across China, valued at tens of millions of US dollars. An ivory carver wrote to say that he has many other types of materials to carve, and he does not want his carving to cost a life. An education official touched by the campaign put the message into the college entrance exam as a Chinese language test, enabling the message to reach nine million college applicants. In four years, the campaign penetrated seventy-five percent of urban China and reduced the group with the most propensities to purchase ivory from fifty-four percent to twenty-six percent.

Grace Ge Gabriel, Yarmouth Port, Massachusetts
Asia Regional Director for the International Fund for Animal Welfare

Being an animal advocate means that at any given moment, strong emotions may take over and potentially threaten the work that needs to be done. The solution for some has been to temporarily set those feelings aside.

Feelings Matter Most of All

You are fearful or want to convey to me that you are afraid. I can't decide. And concerned. You love your dog, you say. Now you tell me how upsetting all of this bite and seizure and shelter hold and Dangerous Dog hearing business is, how you just want it to be over, and how the stress is too much. But you will always love your dog even as you consider the needle for biting. It is a matter, you say, of doing what is right. You feel pressured by the police, neighbors, *your brother to conform. Society demands this, you say. And you must put people first. You want me to be left with the impression that you are a good person—A person who loves his dog. That is very important.*

I listen and try to decide what is genuine and what is ephemeral. You need the approval of a stranger. Why would you care what anyone thinks? I am not indifferent to the animal issue. I demand you place your feelings aside. Discuss your options: a hearing or a probationary stipulation with training. In terms of consequentialism, you did not care when you left the dog alone, did not bother to train him, left the door open when he ran out and bit the neighbor, and now want permission to avoid the responsibility of caring for him. You sit, not at all ashen, and repeat that you don't want to lose your dog as you adjust yourself in the chair. And you feel so sorry.

Where your emotions help with a legal issue, in a custody case or to show valuation of damages for an animal life over that of property based upon a special interspecies relationship, I will listen. Here sympathy obscures the issue. I care about saving your dog, not affect, yet the world that humans form is affect. I tell you that you have agency to make choices for your dog. Sentiment will not save anyone. I recall Hamlet: Thus does conscience make cowards of us all.

I respect my clients enough to take them at their word, often a mistake. You are panicking. I know your stress and what you want above all: to exorcise it by dumping it. You have made up your mind but want me to tell you that stipulating to euthanasia is the right choice. You respond that I am cold when I refuse to agree that death is appropriate resolution. It is noon and you want to be relieved of guilt and are probably thinking of what you will eat for lunch. I smile. Cold, yes I try to be cold. I know the human mind is in constant terror of nonbeing as Sue Grand wrote. That is cold.

When I say that no one cares how you feel, it is because we are here before the law. They may not even be your own. I remind you that litigation is not therapy. I know a well-known psychiatrist who will discuss your feelings with you until you reach a resolution. Not I—I demand a sense of responsibility. We are not convened to mourn future days, but to change the present.

And I never tell you about the suffering I have held in my arms. About the rescues, euthanasias—murders really. The fighting dogs ripped apart. The starving dogs cannibalizing kin. The broken remains of the ritual sacrifices. The shelter smell of fear and bleach, stale death, and the damp floors. The downcast eyes, pools of despair from a subject cast as an empty object in the cruel Master's discourse before the law. I feel all that infinite space but I will never tell you. You that you see the world of animals as a human—the fancy term is anthropocentrism—and claim kinship with your animal, yet now view that kinship as disposable. You must have one feeling not your own, a sense of what your dog feels, alterity is the word here, don't you? Indulge your affect and embrace anticipatory grief or act to change time and fate. Time is out of joint. If you hesitate then you are as damned as your animal is doomed.

Come to terms with your world by changing it, I urge you. Derrida said what the Stoics and the Hebrews said: Take responsibility by acting. So, I ask, will you fight for your dog? Or do you want to talk about your feelings?
John Maher, New York, New York
Professor Emeritus of Animal Law, Touro Law Centre

• • •

I started off in animal rights ten years ago in 2006 when a chance meeting with a long-lost acquaintance led me to visit the crew of the Sea Shepherd vessel the Farley Mowat. The crew was unjustly held hostage in Cape Town Harbour and was in urgent need of food donations. In return for my donation, the captain of the vessel—Alex Cornellisen—gave me a tour of the boat and told me about the plight of the oceans and those who reside within. I carried no knowledge of sealing, whaling, dolphin hunting, or any other issues which befall marine animals. I was shocked by what I heard and felt compelled to do something—anything—to rectify the injustice. I went home and Googled the hell out of animal rights and marine conservation and instantly knew I found my calling. Since that day I have sat on the boards of various organisations, started NGOs, volunteered where I could, travelled the world to document atrocities committed against animals by humans, been their voice in the media, went from eighteen-year-long vegetarian to vegan and eventually became a vegan chef.

In the beginning it was shocking and overwhelming and your own well-being was placed above that of the animals. But the more you grow and learn, the more you realise that your feelings, your emotional and psychological well-being, is secondary to the suffering of the animal. I manage my own emotions by reminding myself that this struggle is not mine, but it is the animals' struggle. This is a gigantic global war against animals with very few soldiers to fight it. We cannot afford the luxury of wallowing in our emotions.

I remember the day it dawned on me. I was watching my first dolphin slaughter at the infamous cove in Taiji. Prior to going to Taiji, I point-blank refused to watch the award-winning documentary, The Cove, *which chronicles this particular dolphin slaughter. I couldn't even watch*

Disney's animated Beauty and the Beast. *It broke my heart and traumatised me when the characters were mean to the Beast.*

Twice in my life I was directly confronted with animal cruelty, and in both instances, my temper allowed me to perform superhuman feats—none of which I remember but which I heard about after the fact. So when I told my family and friends that I was going to hop on a plane and witness the cruelty firsthand, everyone thought I had totally lost the plot. I got all my affairs in order as I was sure that I wasn't coming back and that a Japanese jail would be my home for the next few years. But as I stood on the shore of the cove, hearing the dolphins screaming, their tails slapping the water in panic, and in the throes of death, I was too shocked to move or to react. It was in that moment that I realised that it wasn't about me and my emotions but that it was one hundred percent about the animals. In that moment I decided that the day I put my needs above the needs of the suffering is the day I have not only failed the animals but humanity as well. I never ever want it to be about me, and I intend to honour that promise.

Even though I have personally witnessed the callousness and mercilessness of humanity several times, it never becomes easier. At times the sheer gravity of it is debilitating and overwhelming—but then I remind myself that no matter what I am going through, the animals have it a billion times worse.

If I change the mind and heart of one person, my job is done. Because that one person will change the mind and heart of one person and so the ripple effect extends. If I look back on the status of animal rights as little as five years ago and I look at where we are now, I can clearly see just how fast change has happened. As a vegan I save thousands of *animals. As an activist I share my knowledge. The more people know, the more they are empowered. The more they are empowered, the more they can do.*

I am never beaten down by the abuse I have witnessed. I am however beaten down to the point of deep depression by the actions of those who are supposed to stand together in this fight. The animal advocacy movement is riddled with egos, petty politics, and jealousy. I call it "The Fireman Syndrome." Everyone wants to be the fireman with the kitten in his arms. I also struggle with the notion that we all preach compassion and point fingers at those harming others; we rejoice in instances where a matador is gored to death by his victim. How do we expect people to take our message seriously if we cannot practice what we preach, if we cannot demonstrate to others what compassion should look like? That compassion is unconditional? We walk a very, very thin line in becoming that which we are trying to fight. It is something I struggle with and have to remind myself of daily.

The major hurdle I face is being patient and kind to myself. I don't allow myself the courtesy. I have a job to do, a story to tell, and lives to save.
Nikki Botha, Cape Town, South Africa
Civil Society Activist & Independent Activist

Instead of focusing on what hasn't changed, some advocates focus on the strides that have been made and take pride in what they have been able to accomplish for animals.

As an Animal Liberation activist, I often feel hopelessness, stress, despair, and everything else. I have come to the realization that just as Racism, Sexism, and every other "ism" have never been eradicated, neither will Speciesism be eradicated. Nor can these things be legislated. Sure, legislation can end most, but not all, of the suffering.

My way of dealing with this is to keep in mind that I am really doing all that I can to further the cause. I cannot change everyone. There is no "right approach," and people aren't refusing to go vegan because of us. The fact is that some, probably most, people really don't care about animals. All that we can do is the best we can. Some people are educators, some are Liberators. We need every last approach. And some people cannot be reached. How I avoid being overwhelmed by it all is that I have made these realizations. I do not daydream of the mythical nonviolent/vegan world. I do the very best that I can in this violent and nonvegan world. Taking solace in the fact that at least some animals knew freedom and kindness because some people stood up, stepped forward, and took action for Animal Liberation. Every single animal saved is a battle won.

Derk Brachmann, Manitowoc, Wisconsin

• • •

I have been an animal activist/humane educator for over twenty years. I made the decision to make this my life's work when confronted with all of the horrible ways that animals are cruelly treated and killed behind closed doors on a daily basis. Carrying this awareness of the injustice towards innocent living beings drives me to do the work that I do and be a voice for the voiceless. Every day I have the opportunity to communicate to others and make them aware of the plights of animals used in research, testing, and education either through one-on-one conversations or presentations to a variety of audiences. With each instance I have to discuss my lifestyle as an ethical vegan or to elaborate about the work that I do, it helps me to cope with the awful realities that animals are facing in the world. I am rewarded when I see that aha moment in a person's eyes when they realize that they can do things more humanely after I disclose a disturbing fact about animals or show an image of an individual animal who has been used in research. I carry those moments as personal badges of honor. Those moments help me to move forward and do everything that I can to make a difference for animals in this world.

As a sensitive person, I am saddened when I learn about incidents of animal injustice. I cry when I see a film highlighting any form of animal cruelty. My heart breaks for animals who are treated like a number and not an individual with his or her own unique needs and desires. However, I am able to manage my sadness by steering my thoughts in a positive direction and reminding myself that I have the power to make changes in society by planting seeds of kindness. As the director of a national program that addresses the use of animals in education, I have the opportunity to open people's minds to consider a more humane perspective. I am an optimist and see every interaction that I have with others as a way to motivate myself to make a positive impact on the lives of animals. As a mother with a son on the autism spectrum, I feel that I face more challenging issues in my personal life than I do with work. My work gives me a sense of purpose and in turn gives me hope for the future. I have the ability to mentally push myself through any hardship I face. While things may be difficult in life, I remind myself that no matter how hard things may be for me, there is always someone else dealing with even more difficult circumstances—especially the animals.

Nicole Green, Wyncote, Pennsylvania
Humane Educator/Animal Advocate with an MA in Education and concentration in Humane Education

In order to be effective in this work and not burn out, advocates need to find ways to manage the emotional ups and downs that come with the territory. For some, that means being selective in whom they allow into their lives at any given time.

> *This is the hardest part of the work we do—dealing with the emotions. You have to put your emotions aside and not react to them. The only emotions you can carry around while working is the love for your family and the brotherly love for your fellow rangers.*
>
> *It is very difficult when you find a dead animal that had been killed by people. If it is in a snare hanging from a tree, and seeing the fear that remains on the animal's face or big game that had been hacked to death, with tears that were running from their eyes, you have to hold it in. If you do not and you just react to these emotions, it will result in bigger things that will get you into trouble with the law. I have seen big strong men crying over carcasses of rhinos, elephants, and lions, like it was their children dead on the ground. This kills me on the inside, every time.*
>
> *The worst part is when we have to cut open these magnificent animals to find ballistic proof for the South African Police investigators. It is a long process and can sometimes take up to four hours. Now I want you to put yourself in this position. You are standing next to a rhino you have known for the last three years. She is your pride and joy on the farm. You tell every visitor about her playfulness and her unique personality. Now, she is on her side being cut up into pieces. The person doing the autopsy starts crying and falls down on his knees, holding a small, unborn rhino calf that is already fully formed. Sorry for my language, but that fucks you up for weeks, nonstop. And when you catch the people who did this, you cannot let your emotions take over. You have to*

stay calm and do what you get paid to do: arrest and hand over to the SAPD.

Some of these people get off easy, and you will see them in the streets in less than two weeks. That is when the pictures in your head start playing again, and you relive the moment over again. Yes, you feel what you do is a waste of time some days and that you are not making a difference. But we cannot stop fighting this war against poaching.

We, as Security Rangers, know that if we stop fighting for our wildlife, it will not survive for long. For me, and I believe my fellow Rangers that do this for the love and not for the Rambo Photos, it is a struggle to cope some days. But we support each other to stay strong and sane.

We do not see our families a lot. If we see them for seven days a month, we are lucky. This is difficult, especially if you are married and have children. You do not see them grow up, you are not a part of the life they have, and you cannot expect a one-year-old to understand why you have to do this. Maybe one day, when they are a lot older, they will be able to understand and forgive us for not being there. Not seeing their first steps, not seeing the first time they rode a bike, never seeing the first of anything they did. But we know if we do not do everything we can to save wildlife, that our and your children and grandchildren will go to a museum to see what wildlife used to be. And they will ask us, "Mom, Dad, why did you not stop this?" So before we have to explain that to them, we will stay positive and wake up ready to protect the wildlife that is still alive. GO TO WAR AND WIN!

I have lost a lot of trust in people. Everybody says they will do what they have to and donate and…and…and. But you never hear from them when you need support and funding to get the job done. We are a private organization and do

not get funds from government, so we rely on the support and funding from the public. So when people say "Yes, sure we support what you do and what you want to achieve," I already think to myself, yeah, right. I do not have a lot of time for people. I would rather spend my time with my family and animals. Friends—I have some, do not need more, will consider more if they are for what we do and supportive, not negative about it. But getting people that will give up their lives for real, to save wildlife, is the same as looking for a chicken with teeth.
**Floris Swart, Lydenburg Mpumalanga, South Africa
Founder and CEO, Africa Counter Poaching Federation**

• • •

I was lucky enough to be raised as a vegetarian. My mother taught me at a young age what animals go through when they are slaughtered. I also learnt the law of Karma and from a young schoolchild, I did not want an animal to suffer for my taste buds.

I am a psychologist, currently fighting to get compassion training into schools and integrity leadership workshops for youth. I have a radio and TV slot and try create awareness on the plight on animals wherever I can.

I am currently outraged at the spiraling animal abuse worldwide. Not only is it out of control, but children are starting younger to abuse animals. I am in the process of researching WHERE and HOW can anyone lose their empathy and compassion and inflict pain on a sentient being? If we knew how people become desensitized, we can try rectify and raise consciousness to address this.

My personal feelings about the abuse I see and hear about is rage, hurt, frustration, and huge anger. Not to talk *about sadness and depression. I am concerned that welfare people struggle with Post Traumatic Stress, as I do sometimes. The welfare and rescue people sometimes lose their compassion (compassion fatigue) due to the witnessing of what humans do to animals.*

It has affected me to the point where I have suffered from burn out. I also choose my friends very carefully as I have very little time to give of myself to others. I cut myself off in order to recharge.

At times, the horror out there is overwhelming, and it does feel like it will never improve. Many feel that it's easier if we weren't so compassionate, as we feel deeply and never get over some of the things we witness. But we are proud to do our little bit, as we hope it will have a ripple effect!

It's made me have less respect for humans, as I feel the ugliness outweighs the few kind people helping alleviate the suffering animals, and those that are a voice for them.

I still question, how can humans inflict such pain on animals?

I will never give up fighting for them, one way or another.
Charissa Bloomberg, Cape Town, South Africa
Celebrity Psychologist

While there is no one coping strategy that will work for everyone, you might get a couple of ideas from the advocates below.

"I'm a freak." That's how one friend succinctly summarized her experience as a vegan and animal advocate in a decidedly nonvegan world. As an animal and environmental advocate and a vegan myself, I can empathize with the feeling— one that most vegans will have to come to terms with living in a decidedly nonvegan world.

As the leader of a large nonprofit animal protection organization, I am privy to the details of unimaginable suffering of animals. There often seems to be no end to the numbers of animals involved or the magnitude of their suffering. At times, I have felt close to despair. The feeling is a mixture of frustration, anger, and sadness that can be overwhelming. How does one continue to go about their life day to day when they know that at any given moment millions of animals are being kicked, disfigured, burned, ground up, chained, fought, neglected, and starved, often times with the blessing of our own laws?

The answer for me is twofold. First, I surround myself with compassionate friends and colleagues. I am fortunate to have made a career of fighting for justice for animals, but even if I hadn't, I would be involved as a volunteer with animal protection causes. I would seek and sustain myself by working common cause with people who understand.

Second, for me, is humor. It may seem counterintuitive to find humor in the midst of overwhelming suffering. But without it, I would not be able to continue to fight for animals. I would likely succumb to bitterness, depression, or despair. None of which would help animals. Having a sense of humor allows me to release anger and despair in favor of laughter, whether laughing at absurdity, my own foibles, or making someone else laugh. Humor also makes me a better advocate. Animal advocates need to be persuasive. And people are not persuaded by glum, angry, or bitter people.

Stephen Wells, Cotati, California
Executive Director, Animal Legal Defense Fund

• • •

Using the law to change animals' conditions: the story of an Italian animal law lawyer

I'm Carla Campanaro. I'm an Italian lawyer, thirty-five years old, and I have been working in LAV as the head of LAV Legal Office for ten years. Lav is one of the most important Italian NGOs which have been fighting for forty years for animal rights (www.lav.it) and to protect all the species of animals.

It has been ten years that I've worked as a lawyer for animal rights, and in these years I have seen all kinds of mistreatment, abuse on all kind of animals, trying with all my efforts and work to stop it.

I think that the way I became an animal law lawyer was born from my big compassion for animal needs. The more I was suffering by watching or seeing animal abuse, the more I wanted to be useful in protecting them, as far as possible. That's why, maybe, despite that in my work I only see animal pain and killing, I find the strength to go on, because my objective is to change things. Sometimes, when I suffer watching mistreatments, I tell myself that I'd suffer more if I didn't do anything useful to prevent it.

During my trials and my work, I often feel rage for what I discover caused the behavior of the abuser, but this gives me more strength to resist and win my trials. I'm an optimistic person, and I believe that winning even one case can change the minds of the people. That's why I never feel my work is futile. What I do to survive all the suffering and pain I always see is working with a big team of people I really trust, with whom I can talk of my feelings, beyond the work, and to find the common strength to win and save more animals, as far as possible. Another thing I do is I try as much as possible not to focus all my life on my work and consequently, on the animal suffering. I try to have other interests and hobbies, as for example, photography.

During my trials, and particularly during the hearings, I often suffer. I live personally all what happens, and I feel responsible for the lives of the animals I try to protect with their sequestration related to the trial. That's why I'm really drained, but when I win (and I win often, maybe because I put inside the right energy), I'm the happiest person in the world, and I feel that all my efforts have been repaid. Here you can see one of the trials I won, saving the lives of 3000 beagles destined to vivisection (http://www.lav.it/en// green-hill-appellate-court.
Carla Campanaro, Rome, Italy
LAV (www.lav.it), Chief of LAV legal office, lawyer in animal law, and PhD in European environmental law

• • •

I wanted to express that while bearing witness to the horrors that are involved with animal advocacy and yes dealing with the frustrations that the legal system and the public can bring, I have found that the majority of the AR community has been supportive of me and my work. To be honest, I personally use whatever frustration, negativity, defeatist or combative attitudes I encounter to fuel me as opposed to bringing me down, and that goes for within the AR community and outside of it, i.e., in school, in my work, etc. For me, as long as I know I am doing my best and doing what I know in my heart is right, people can say or do whatever they please, I have learned that I cannot control how others react, only how I act and react to situations. Being and feeling depressed or frustrated, or allowing the ugliness of the world to get you down, is counterproductive in my mind. You have to find a way to move past it and continue to fight the injustices you see, and if you are weakened by them, then you are no use to the many that need you to speak for them. Do I get angry? Of course, I am only human. But to be honest, I have never felt so much anger that it was overwhelming to me and especially not towards my fellow advocates.

In the big picture of things, we are all working for the same goal. I may not always agree with their methods, or we may not all share the same outlooks as far as animal welfare vs. animal rights per se but I have found most to be accepting of my message, regardless. For me being vegan and an advocate means trying to do as little harm as possible to another living being, and you cannot do that if you are not willing to learn from others and listen with an open mind and heart. Words as well as actions can be hurtful, and I make a conscious choice to not surround myself with those that would intentionally hurt another person, with either. I do not participate in toxic friendships, so for me, my experiences with negativity amongst my fellow advocates is few and far between. Do I see it around me, yes of course, but I choose to not participate in it. As far as the anger and frustration I feel when I see or hear the horrific acts that animals are put through daily or with the slow pace that legislation can move at or the frustration in waiting for someone to have their own ah-ha moment and get on board and support what needs to be done, it definitely can play on your emotions, but as I mentioned prior, I may be angered/frustrated by the situation, circumstances, act, etc., but it is not an "overwhelming" feeling of any kind; disheartening, sad, downright sickening at times, yes all of the above, but not an overwhelming challenge.

I personally have my own coping mechanisms and venting tools that I use, and I think it's important that everyone find what is theirs. Everyone should have a way to release those feelings that can weigh heavy on your heart and mind,

as opposed to releasing them negatively or bottling them up inside to where they interfere with your own health and well-being. I personally vent by writing and then use that feeling to fuel me to keep fighting.
Thomas Ponce, Florida
President and Founder, Lobby for Animals

• • •

Of all the animal cruelty and abuse I have seen, whether firsthand or on footage gathered by investigators, the one that sticks with me most is the one that was easiest to watch. It isn't one showing the obscene violence of an individual human or an individual animal or graphic slaughter footage or the institutionalized cruelty of factory farming or one of the countless other examples of abuse that make you wish you could erase the images from your mind.

For me, it is a film of fluffy, two day old chicks, on a conveyor belt. They ride the conveyor belt to the end and then drop in batches into boxes, ready to shipped off for fattening at industrial farms. It is a very strange thing to watch, a factory production line, with tiny creatures in the place of clanking bottles or tin cans. It is the idea it captures—that these sentient creatures have become just another part of a production machine—that haunts me.

As my years working in animal welfare have gone on, I have developed effective "blinkers" for watching animal suffering—an imaginary filter I put over my eyes that allows me to look for the information I need: who is doing this, where is it, how does it breach legislation, how can I make it stop. Even with those blinkers on, it would not be manageable without the ability to try to do something about it, and I am incredibly lucky that my job gives me that. I have a collection of films of humans helping animals that I watch after viewing anything very distressing, to "cleanse my eyeballs."

Working in this field changes the way you view the world and the relative place of humans and animals within it. More and more I see the extent to which people will close their eyes to suffering or be willfully ignorant of it. I see people who are devastated by the loss of a beloved pet, who will console themselves with a meal of factory-farmed sausages. Or who give their time and money to save tigers from poaching and then have holiday pictures taken with chained tigers to show their friends. I conclude that we are a very strange species, capable of both great compassion and great cruelty, often demonstrated by the same person at the same time.
Emma Slawinski, European Programmes Director—World Animal Protection, formerly Head of Campaigns—Compassion in World Farming

• • •

My main focus in my work is farm animals. I have a seven-year background as a meat inspector at slaughterhouses (abattoirs) around South Africa. To me, what is most frustrating is how slow things happen/take place. I do depend on my Spirituality a lot (Christian) and also do a lot of exercise.

Around fifty percent of the time, my personal concern/frustration is when I can't seem to change/influence my immediate family, then I ask, "who out there would listen or heed the call?" But at other times, I will get an odd email/SMS about someone who has changed because of hearing my talk on radio or seeing an article in a newspaper.

I feel I have now been "desensitized." I have seen and heard a lot over the years (I must say I am bothered but not to such an extent that I will close my eyes and look away).

Perhaps the biggest hurdle I face in my work is that I can't set achievable goals within the time frame I want; the work always depends on the people/organisations I engage with.

I don't have an issue with people or how I see the world. There are times I feel like I am neglecting my family and am being away a lot, but when I sit down, I see that the most would be three days a month that I will be away.

After doing this work for years, I find I've become more kinder towards people; I am now a "conscious" eater, and have developed patience.
Anonymous, South Africa

6
Serving the Sentient

It is more important to prevent animal suffering, rather than sit to contemplate the evils of the universe praying in the company of priests.

— *Buddha*

- Tending to the lacerations of an abused elephant
- Lassoing a mangy, starving dog
- Watching another healthy cat be euthanized
- Filming the death throes of a pig

THESE ARE THE experiences of the multitudes that devote their lives to helping animals: the veterinarians, rescuers, shelter workers, and undercover investigators at slaughterhouses and factory farms. With fervor and commitment, these are the people who face brutality head on, the ones who offer their bodies, minds, and hearts to champion the needs of the silent majority. But might these animal protagonists be contending with their own burdens unbeknown to most?

Succoring
All veterinarians have a hard but vital job ministering to the needs of the sick and wounded. But the cadre of vets who work with rescued companion animals, who tend to the casualties of war and natural disasters, who treat the victims of wildlife atrocities such as poaching and captivity, or who look after animals in countries without any animal-protection laws, are often confronted with injuries, abuse, and neglect on a far greater scale than that seen in traditional veterinary practices. The mangled face of the victim of a dog-fighting ring; the abandoned zoo animals in a war-torn city, shrapnel lodged in their emaciated bodies; the donkey blinded for not being able to carry his heavy load; the charred fur of a rabbit, a marginalized victim of domestic violence; or the lone, stressed shark swimming nowhere in a tiny glass enclosure as he entertains tourists in a luxury hotel—none of these situations would shock these veterinarians. Seeing firsthand the violence and disregard exhibited toward these animals can take its toll on these healers. Anger at the perpetrators and deep sadness for the victims can, over time, result in practitioners who themselves become emotionally scarred by their experience, a situation often referred to as compassion fatigue.

Elizabeth Strand states that "the biggest contributor to compassion fatigue in veterinary medicine is moral stress. Moral stress is when you're aware of what ethical principles are at stake, but external factors prevent you from doing (something). Moral stress is unique and insidious in that it cannot be alleviated by normal means of stress management. It arises among people whose life work is aimed at promoting the well-being of animals" (as cited in Kahler, 2015).

> *I can't say when exactly my love for animals began. I would say that I was born like that.*
>
> *From my earliest memories, I have always been surrounded by many types of animals. I loved going to my grandma's to play with the toads and crabs, and if there was a stray*

dog, I would reach out to him and just hug or kiss him. I am lucky my parents never said no to that as I always had a kind of connection to the animals. But there have been times when I wish I hadn't, because it hurts.

During school, they always asked me what I wanted to be when I grew up and the obvious answer was "a vet." Little did I know about the pain and the tears I would shed. I studied so hard to save lives. And when you graduate as a vet you are so joyful, until you see that first patient—the one that bursts the bubble. That's the patient whose family doesn't care, won't pay for the treatment, or is too tired to look after him/her. That is a breaking point, because you are faced with what society really is about—a bunch of selfish apes.

Then one day it all started: a dog was being kicked by some drunks, and I had to do something about it. I got out of my car and picked up the thirty kilo golden retriever and took him with me. From that day on, I rescued and found homes for many dogs. It is exhausting. Not everyone wants a dog that's not purebred, that is ugly, or is full grown.

If you ask me how I deal with the feelings, well, I don't know. I cry, a lot. I have woken up some days and laid in bed crying, because this world is too evil for me. I can't understand how anyone could harm a baby cat or baby orangutan. It is hard for me to understand humans, and many times I feel like I am not one.

I get angry at people, but I have chosen not to fill myself with hatred. How stupid are you to leave a dog inside a car in hot weather? How stupid are you to chain up your dog and leave it outside during a snowstorm. I always ask people, "Would you do that to a three year old kid?" They immediately say NO, and then I would say, "Then why do you do it to a dog?"

I just got back from working on a ground zero area after an earthquake. We were part of the relief efforts for the nonhuman victims. If I could tell you all the stories about abused and sick animals, if I showed you the pictures, you would probably have nightmares. Then you have to look at these animals' eyes and tell him/her that not all humans are like that. I often apologize to them; I ask for forgiveness as my species walks around causing pain and destruction.

It got so overwhelming that I had to stop doing that, and so I walked away and moved into direct action animal activism. That has given me some good days, but little did I know that I would face evil in its worst way. I have the faces of the animals I have seen dead recorded in my mind—all the ones I wasn't able to save. I wish sometimes I was disconnected from all of this and that I had a life with family and happy thoughts. But then I see an animal suffer, and I get up to do something about it.

I look back and see how much of my life has changed, how much of myself has changed. It's a lonely life, and you just wonder to yourself if you are so wrong, as society seems to punish you, especially in a third world country. So I have become a "hamster," as I like to call myself. I avoid meeting people, especially men, because I know my vegan activist life will be an issue, and I don't feel like explaining why I do what I do. I stay home and do what hamsters do, only I don't have a wheel. Hahaha.

I have this shield, pretending I never wanted to get married, have children, or a boyfriend. You know why? Because it's better to pretend than to face the reality and explain things to people. People see me as this tough, hard-core independent woman who likes to be alone and needs no one. But the truth is so different. The truth is, I cry when I am

alone and I am scared and I wish I had someone by my side to protect me once in a while. Being a protector is exhausting.
Maria Cristina Cely Cajas, DVM, Quito, Ecuador
Volunteer for Darwin Animal Doctors and Sea Shepherd Conservation Society

Focusing on what they are able to control and whom they are able to help is what helps keep these veterinarians going.

Growing up in Brooklyn, I did a lot of rescuing as a kid. Any stray kittens that sis and I could find we would take in and find them homes. But I wanted to do more when I saw an injured or sick stray. That is what inspired me to be a veterinarian. Throughout vet school in the Caribbean, I also continued to find many strays and got them adopted or sent to the states to find permanent homes. Once I received my degree, I set forth to look for vet work in animal hospitals. The first year wasn't rewarding enough until I was offered a position as head shelter vet at the SPCA of Westchester. This was the real eye-opener and the biggest change of my life. I'll never forget my first cruelty case when an animal control officer brought in a Pit. He arrived with a swollen head and ruptured eye, due to being hit with a hard object. All he wanted to do was sit in my lap and lick my face. He was admitted under my care and recovered but was blind in that eye. I had emotions of stress and sadness to see an animal in that state still want human affection. But it was all worth it when he found his forever loving home eight months later.

From that day on, I dedicated my life to helping several shelters. I stayed with SPCA for six years and ventured to closer ones in NYC, such as ASPCA and ACC. I learned the hard way at ACC that I couldn't save them all though. I remember being greeted by a friendly Pit with all tail wags and kisses in the hallway of this high kill shelter. I asked the kennel attendant where he was taking him. He said, "His time is up." I'll never forget that day and how devastated I was. How could they just dispose of a sweet and friendly dog? I immediately told them to give that dog another day. I learned the hard way the next day. I was in charge of 80 dogs and one hundred cats on a daily basis. I made sure not only that they received medical care but that they had fresh water, food, and clean bedding. I couldn't keep up, and every day, I was let down. So many animals were surrendered to this kill shelter by owners or claims of being strays. I had compassion fatigue and was finally burnt-out. I had to make changes to my life, or depression would set in.

Within some time, I managed to open my own veterinary hospital. This gave me the opportunity to be able to work with the other side—the rescues. I was more than happy to offer my vet services at very low rates to these stray animals in need. They either came from kill shelters, owner surrenders, or streets of NYC. I made a promise that I would never let another animal be euthanized because he/she was homeless. As a result, I have offered to do adoptions at my clinic. This has been one of the most rewarding experiences—to see an unwanted or abused pet find a forever loving home.
Yvonne Szacki, DVM, Brooklyn, New York

• • •

I have been a veterinarian for thirty years and in the animal field for approximately forty. I have traveled the world and seen a great deal of animal suffering and abuse. Now as a holistic veterinarian for over twenty years, I have seen thousands of animals suffer and die due to the greed of the pharmaceutical companies and the conventional veterinarians who buy into their propaganda and what I believe should be considered malpractice in the veterinary field. I became a vegetarian at seventeen and have had many challenges during the decades of my life. The natures of my struggles have shifted during the years.

With the passing of time and the accumulation of wisdom, what I have learned is that the battle is really an internal one. I am in charge of deciding what to focus on. I am in charge of where to allocate my energies. My business is to do my job to the best of my ability with the knowledge that I have acquired. I cannot fix the world. I cannot let seemingly horrific injustices get me down. Alongside of my deep love of animals, I have a deep faith in a Divine force. I believe that God is ultimately in charge, and it is my dharma (righteous duty) that I must focus on and to leave the rest to God. I must mind my business and let God take care of His/Her business.

Here is a story that I love, and I hope you will too. It has been told in various forms by many people and is adapted from "The Star Thrower," by Loren Eiseley (1907–1977).

A small boy is walking along a beach one morning, and he sees the vast beach littered with thousands and thousands of starfish that had washed ashore. In the distance the boy sees an old man walking along very slowly and bending down continually to throw something into the sea. As the boy gets closer, he sees the old man is picking up each starfish and gently tossing it back into the ocean. The boy asks his elder why he is doing this. The old man replies, "When the sun comes up and the tide goes out, they will die because they cannot get back into the water by themselves."

The young boy tauntingly replied, "You are a fool. There are miles and miles of beach with tens of thousands of starfish. Even if you work all day, your effort won't make any difference at all."

The old man listened calmly and bent down and picked up yet another starfish and threw it into the sea. "It made a difference to that one," said he and continued walking.

As the saying goes: "It is better to light one candle than curse the darkness."
Marcie Fallek, DVM, Fairfield, Connecticut

Saving

Stepping out of your truck into the pitch-black night, you spy the pacing dog off in the distance, enclosed behind a barbed wire fence. You've cased the place several times before, so you know the lay of the land. Based on an anonymous tip, you know the growling canine was left to fend for himself over a week ago when the owners of the now defunct scrap metal shop he's been guarding closed down. They're called "junkyard dogs," and you've met many of them throughout the years as an animal rescuer. You're a professional—you have the tools, the gear, and the will to get the job done. But you're also seasoned enough to appreciate the unpredictability of these situations. The dog is likely frightened and might lunge and attack, seriously injuring you. Or he might run behind a narrow enclosure, making it difficult to get at him. How then do you draw him out? Someone might come along to make trouble for you. During these times, fear, stress, anger, and sadness are often along for the ride. Stories like this and worse abound within the animal-rescue community. Moreover, the emotional ups and downs and major time commitment intrinsic to rescue can make having a balanced personal life quite challenging for some.

Have you ever heard of the old adage "Be careful what you wish for because you just might get it?" When I was in my early 20s, I told my friend that I wanted to have lots of property and take care of hundreds of rescue animals in need. Decades later, I look back at the naiveté of my dream.

Today I am the Executive Director of Mighty Mutts. We are a not for profit, all volunteer, no kill animal rescue organization and one of the largest in the country. My involvement with this organization started with a mere donation of medicines. My first rescue dog had passed away, and I didn't want the expensive medication to go to waste. From the first day of the medicine drop off, my life changed forever. Over a fifteen-year period, I have been immersed in the horrors of the animal rescue world. Week after week, I watched our founder bringing newly rescued dogs and cats to be shown for adoption. These animals had been thrown out of cars, hung from trees, burned, beaten, used as bait for dog fighting rings, devocalized (where the vocal chords are removed so no one can hear them bark), starved, and violated in every vile way possible.

My faith in humanity diminished on a daily basis. In addition to every form of torture that I witnessed, I had to deal with the lying public. People would concoct dozens of reasons as to why they were dumping their animals. These animals meant nothing more to them than a new pair of shoes that were discarded at the end of the season. People typically didn't want to pay for food or veterinary care any longer or would decide to have a baby and make that their new focus.

The more I saw, the deeper I got into the actual rescue process itself. My focus became Pit Bulls when I took in a foster named Angelique. I, of course, ended up adopting her since she did not receive one application for adoption. Angelique was starved and beaten in the eye with a two by four and left to bleed to death in the street. She clearly had been used for breeding multiple times. It became my mission to change the perception of this breed and put the focus on the actual problem, which is horrible owners manipulating these poor dogs for bad purposes. I actually started to put myself in life risking situations. Friends of mine told me that I could literally die if I continued going into these dangerous areas trying to deal with criminals.

Before I entered the rescue world, I went out like most people do. I made plans and showed up. I traveled. I actually had some type of balance in my life. Now, every time the phone rings, it's someone that needs something, and they want it done immediately to unburden themselves. My pure moments of joy are few and far between. They come when we find that wonderful adoptive home. I am also incredibly proud of the amazing volunteers that open their hearts as well to help. We all look at these animals as our children that we want to protect for a lifetime.

My hope is continued education for the public and that stronger laws will be enacted to punish abusers. Until those goals are met, I will continue in my mission and dream of an actual week at the beach. Please **visit mightymutts.org** if you are interested in donating, fostering, adopting, or volunteering.

Michelle Marlowe, New York, New York

• • •

Animal rescue has been a big part of our lives for close to thirty years. What started out as a love for animals has turned into a lifetime commitment to helping those in need. We realized quickly that once we become involved with animal rescue, there was no turning back. We bonded quickly to people that shared our love and concern for the innocent animals that needed someone to stand up for them. Without realizing it, we became inundated with animal situations that we could not turn our backs on. Some rescues were easy, but some required having to confront nasty and dangerous people. We found ourselves entering dangerous neighborhoods and having to sweet talk people into allowing us to help an animal that was in their possession. At times it was hard to hold back our feelings, but we knew that if we said one thing out of line, it could ruin our chances of helping an animal.

Animal rescue is also an emotional roller coaster; you can be high as a kite one minute and as low as can be the next minute. Sometimes you have to make decisions as to what rescue is more important and more feasible and then feeling awful about the rescue you were unable to do. It is a balancing act that is not always easy to deal with. The rewards of rescuing are the incredible feeling you get when you finally match the right animal with the right person and they have found their forever home or when you rescue an animal from a horrible situation and know that they are now safe and can begin a new life. All in all, animal rescue is extremely fulfilling as long as you're prepared for the sacrifice of any semblance of a normal life and the emotional tug-of-war that it puts you through.

Paul and Doreen Eiseman, Flushing, New York
Loving Touch, Inc., Paul Eiseman, President/Doreen Eiseman, Board Member

• • •

I can tell you from my own experience as the founder/director of a rescue, there are times when I feel very alone in spite of the 300-plus volunteers I have amassed. I struggle to do the things that are necessary to keep the rescue running—squeezing that work into time that should be spent at my actual work or with my family or just plain sleeping or eating, pushing myself to a point beyond exhaustion and wearing *my mental and physical health down. My own animals, my family, my work, my health, my finances all suffer because of the passion I feel toward my "mission" to save the lives of animals I don't even know.*

Rescue is not for the weak. A rescuer must be able to withstand a roller coaster of emotions, from the elation of a last minute save or a perfect adoption to the loss of a life fought for but not won. Depression and rejection, abject sadness...all a daily fact of life and death. But those of us who stay with it are in it for the win—the beating heart. My husband says that I am online all the time, and we pretend that I'm playing an online game (he is into online PVP games)—we call it "dogging," and when I win, the dog lives.

All of this is enough of a drain emotionally that I don't even need to get into the drama that rescuers create amongst themselves. I don't have time for that. I try to be tolerant of others, allow for my own bad days, considerate of the situations other rescuers are struggling with, leading to the decisions they make and understanding that mistakes happen in an imperfect world. There is never enough time, never enough money, never enough volunteers/fosters.
Jen McFadden, Red Bank, New Jersey
Home Free Animal Rescue

Rescuing an animal isn't always possible, and having to face that reality can be hard to bear. For some people, that feeling of powerlessness spurs them on to become animal rescuers.

Approximately thirty-five years ago I was hired as an office assistant to a research scientist. Being very young, I had had no clue what animal research meant. Rats, rabbits, and dogs were basically used, abused, and then done away with (killed). One day two research assistants asked for my help.

They said they couldn't get a rabbit out of "its" cage. The rabbit was resisting being picked up. Would I help? they queried. When I entered the laboratory I saw this little trembling being, eyes big with terror, body twisted with fear. At that moment, I felt helpless. What could I do? I quit the job and decided that whatever I did in life, it would include helping animals however I could.

Shortly after this I came across a stray dog who became my first rescued dog. I named him Baby Bear. As the years went by, many stray dogs graced my life. I was grateful for seeing the horror of animal abuse in that research lab because it gave me the impetus to become a rescue person.

Little has changed since that time. We still torture animals in labs, on factory farms and breeding facilities, etc. And all this is due to the human need to dominate Nature. Indeed we are losing our precious planet Earth because of this need to dominate. It is deeply troubling to me, but I find reason to continue whenever I look into the eyes of the animals. They are like water: pure, open, and forgiving.
Sharon Azar, Brooklyn, New York

Of course animal rescue can also be a much more protracted and circuitous endeavor when rescuing animals hinges on collaboration with a variety of stakeholders. For example, consider those who rescue bears from the bile farms, which are prevalent in China, Vietnam, and Laos. The rescuers can document the abuses on the farms, but to actually remove the bears, relationships must first be forged with government officials who have the power to outlaw the practice. Simultaneously, outreach to the public is necessary to put pressure on those officials to change existing legislation. Suggesting and/or offering the farms' proprietors alternative ways to make a living can make them more amenable to a change in livelihood. Finally, sanctuaries must be built to house the rescued bears. One can imagine all the intense emotions that arise as a result of making this type of rescue a reality. Trying to navigate the rescue of animals when you're based in a different city or country can also be complicated.

> The animal abuse in Iran can be overwhelming, causing feelings of helplessness, anger, and frustration as there is no support by authorities; they are clueless about the situation and believe killing dogs actually solves the population control. I feel we never do enough, and the work we are able to do barely makes a dent with over 700 dogs at the shelter.
>
> I believe I am making a small difference but not even close to the difference I'd like to make. If I can find a way to implement a spay/neuter/release program (while living in the United States) in Iran, in a country that is so lost and so far behind, I will begin to see the light at the end of the tunnel.
>
> I am lucky I don't live in Iran and do not have to endure the abuse firsthand—although I have seen enough pictures and read enough notes from our team—that I can only imagine what it feels like to run into these cases on a daily basis.
>
> I wish others could commit, follow through, or simply trust my expertise and knowledge in this field, to make rescuing and fostering easier on not just the dog but the people involved. Also, I hope people can one day remove emotion from the situation and stay focused on the end goal—safety and happiness for the dog. When emotions run high, it is very difficult for people to respond logically; rather they react emotionally, causing miscommunication and sometimes arguments. The amount of time, energy, and resources needed to assist one dog out of Iran can be overwhelming. So I remind myself "one dog at a time" can, and will, eventually effect change for the better.

> Because my husband is not a "dog person," he doesn't understand why I give so much of my time to rescue. I work full time, do rescue work full time, and take care of our rescue dog full time, all on my own, as my husband prefers to not be involved. And amid all of this, of course I need to spend time with my husband as well.
>
> Sometimes it's hard to interact with people as they expect me to help ALL rescue groups in Iran and not just one. When I don't help, I'm made to feel like the bad guy. I always try to explain to them that every group has so much on their plates; why not have more than one group, but that can fall on deaf ears.
>
> I've become stronger dealing with the tough cases, learned how to deal with people in a diplomatic way, although my straightforward responses ticks people off at times, still.
>
> **Farah Ravon, San Jose, California**
> **Vafa Animal Shelter—Foreign Adoptions**

For change to happen, we need to be cognizant of how our beliefs and actions have the potential to negatively impact the culture's less powerful groups: both animals and people.

> It's quite frustrating. The more I know and observe as a vegan and a cat rescue advocate about how humans mistreat animals, the more frustrated, sad, and angry I get. When I know that people will kick and torture animals in the food industry, when I see that people pit acid on a cat's face and kids battering a helpless cat with a metal rod, I quickly lose my faith in humanity. In some ways I'm not surprised about the increase in racial violence in recent months because I always think that if humans do that to someone helpless, they will certainly do that to each other.

It also feels like it's never-ending work and that we are barely making a dent. I see an extremely hardworking few who scrape together their dollars for vet bills, work full time, and rescue in their personal time. These few have to make up for the many who cause a lot of the issues to begin with, not spaying and neutering, throwing out their cat because they got bored. And I wonder, why do people think lives are objects? Maybe it's because we live in a disposable society. Plastic cups, paper plates, everything is made to easily toss.

I have to make a concerted effort to see the good, otherwise it would just overwhelm me. I reach out and connect with other vegans and other rescuers so that I can see that even though I have lost my faith in humanity as a whole, that individuals within it are amazing, kind, and caring. They give of themselves selflessly to make a difference in the lives of animals. And if enough people can start thinking like that then humanity may just have a chance in the future.

Someone I know recently listed a video on social media. It was a video of little boy in front of a low hung piñata. The adults around him are urging him to hit the piñata as hard as he can. He holds the bat and stands there. Then he puts the bat down, runs up to the piñata, hugs it, and starts to cry. The adults all laugh. The person who posted this commented that he was laughing so hard when he saw this. I commented gently that if more people were like this little boy, we wouldn't have all the violence and shootings that we had these last few weeks. This summarizes our society today and the way most people think. Most kids inherently do not want violence, but the adults instill that in them and ridicule kindness and caring. It's really sad.

Hazel, New York

Caretaking

The black dog with the gray beard plops down on the floor beside his well-dressed young guardians, who explain to the receptionist he's gotten too old to be a playmate for their kids. A gaunt cat with mangled back paws lies whimpering in the filthy cardboard box left outside the door. Into the building comes a young man who drags a young dog, tail between her legs, across the floor. Covered with scabs and bite marks, the dog urinates as his guardian drops the leash and runs out shouting that he has no use for the dog. Long-haired feline siblings with big blue eyes are deposited at the front desk. The woman tearfully says her new boyfriend hates all cats. Just another day at the animal shelter. Who will live, and who will die? Who will be adopted and how soon? These are questions that those who work at animal shelters grapple with on a daily basis. Some people are fortunate to work at shelters that have adequate resources for the animals and a high adoption rate. Others, however, work at open-admission shelters where whether young or old, healthy or infirm, a majority of the animals will be euthanized. Often these open-admission shelters have insufficient funding, which translates into limited resources and staff to attend to both the physical and emotional needs of the animals. Regardless of the type and conditions of the animal shelter, it's understandable how those who work there might be emotionally impacted by both the physical and mental conditions of the animals brought in, as well as the sheer number of animals that walk in, are dragged to, or dumped at their doors.

> *Playing beat the clock with life and death and death always winning.*
>
> *That was my experience working at the local city kill shelter. Every morning, I'd walk the wards, and my heart would literally hurt. I was overwhelmed by the sounds of dogs begging for their lives, hoping to be noticed by anyone entering the room. Watching the sick ones coughing, to the point I thought they'd die, was excruciating for me!*

Seeing and smelling kennels with bloody feces all over the floor and all over the paws of the dogs that inhabited them made my stomach turn. Within a few minutes, I'd find myself overcome with emotion and smell, equally. Tears would roll down my cheeks as I'd make promises to all of my caged friends that I would get them out—liberate them once and for all! Being claustrophobic only compounded my discomfort because I could see that animals can and do indeed suffer from this condition too, and I felt like I was absorbing their anxiety.

On these walks, I'd take my trusty little notepad and frantically write myself descriptive notes. While navigating my way through this hellhole that masquerades as a shelter, I'd try to spend a few minutes at each cage in an effort to come up with a special word or phrase to help me remember each of the animals when I got back to my desk so I could send out 500 e-mails to all my contacts with hopes of saving some lives with the stories I'd create. While standing outside these cages reading their kennel cards, I'd put my fingers in between the cold, poop smeared bars and try to pet a head or rub a nose to, in some small way, provide a second of comfort and love to these wonderful creatures.

My e-mails were so powerful that many of my friends told me they couldn't get through them without crying. I said that was the goal and hoped they'd take those tears and convert them into desire to help! Many did! I was very successful in getting folks interested in adopting. However, way too often, when I'd go into the computer to write a note indicating I had an adopter, I'd almost always find out the animals I could have saved was already in the FREEZER! Time and time again, I lost. The pain of losing was like no other—a combination of outrage, disgust, and defeat! So many times I found myself saying, "I was this close, dammit!"

> *I could feel myself beginning to unravel. I was obsessed with what I saw during the day, and each night I would awaken to the memory of a dog or cat that I had made friends with over the course of the previous few days that had been killed. I'd find myself waking up crying; I was tormented. It boggled my mind that people worked in this kind of environment for years and years. As I watched them, I was embarrassed and disappointed that I couldn't get through any given day without crying multiple times, and yet these people who were making the actual decisions on who would die today and who would tomorrow, and the people who carried out the slaughter, shed no tears. How was this possible? How could any human being NOT HURT? I just didn't get it.*
>
> *Each day as I exited my car in the parking lot and walked into that God-awful building with so few opportunities for animals to make it out alive, I'd be filled with dread. The only consolation I had was saving a pet here and there.*
>
> **Mary Jo Tobin, Brooklyn, New York**

However, the often difficult and draining nature of the work does not preclude some shelter workers from enjoying and taking pride in what they do. These individuals are able to focus all their energy on helping as many animals as possible, while still acknowledging their limitations.

> *Every day, I fluctuate between a mixture of sadness, frustration, and stress, sometimes anger, at the amount of unwanted animals that come in our doors every day, and I'm sad to have them spend any amount of time behind kennel bars. But at the same time, I am grateful that I am here working tirelessly to place them in new homes, grateful that I love what I do, and I feel proud to do work that makes*

such a direct, palpable difference in animals' lives day in and day out.

I get frustrated with the irresponsibility of some pet owners, their lack of knowledge/patience/understanding sometimes about what it takes to love and care for a pet for life, but I never deem my efforts futile. I know wholeheartedly that my job is tough sometimes, but I know that I make a difference for those that come into the shelter and whom I am able to help. I will always believe that it is worth making a difference for even one animal even if I can't help all of them. It sure makes a difference for those ones who do find new fosters/homes.

When I find myself feeling particularly emotional or upset or stressed by the work, I do my best to remember that I do make a difference, that my work matters, and if I wasn't here, then I wouldn't be helping at all. That usually keeps me going—that and taking time to enjoy the simple joys of life, like chilling with my boyfriend and watching TV and relaxing, doing yoga, adhering to a vegan lifestyle, hanging with friends, and talking about it when I'm stressed. It's important to take time to take care of yourself, especially if you have a stressful job like this, working in animal welfare, and I do my best to pay attention to that regularly.

Coping with the fact that you simply can't find placement for every animal all the time, you have to balance what you can do with what you know is the impossibility of finding new homes for everyone. And trying to have patience and better understanding when people come to surrender their pets.

I do work long hours sometimes, but it's truly a labor of love, so sometimes I get stressed when having to work late, but at the end of the day I'm thankful I love my work.

Working in animal welfare sometimes changes your views of pet owners; it makes you frustrated and angry when people don't care for them properly or if they abuse them. That is particularly hard and can make you have a negative view of humanity and how we treat animals. But I focus on the good people who care for them, people who work with me, and the adopters/volunteers/rescue partners who find new homes for them. That improves my interactions with people when I focus on the good.

I've gotten better at my job over the years, built and maintained excellent relationships in the animal welfare world, and working so long in animal welfare has definitely influenced my decision to become vegan. I've been vegan since 2013 and have never felt healthier or more in line with my ethics and values.

Jessica, New York, New York

• • •

Ever since a very small child, I couldn't keep my hands off animals. All types. Initially we couldn't have animals of our own, so I befriended a stray feral cat, named him Shadow, and used my allowance to buy him food. He became tolerant of me touching him, and it was a great joy. All I wanted was a horse and a dog. My dad would say, "Someday, honey, you'll have lots of horses and dogs." He spoke that over my life often! Little did he know where those words would take me. He never got to see the fruit as he left us much too early. I'm sure he smiles often as he watches us—no doubt in my mind about that.

I volunteered at a local shelter that was very small, but received 1,000 cats and kittens a month during kitten season. It was my first look at the sad reality of how many animals were homeless.

I rescued one by one in college, graduated, and came back home to teach. I took in my first "heart dog"; she came to school with me and had my heart tight in her soft and knowing eyes.

Then started as a Vet Tech at a local vet. During those eight years, I was blessed to begin relationships with many different rescue people and countless animals of all types.

I was interested in helping Greyhounds and rescued them for twelve years. Then we took in orphan Pit Bull/Greyhound mix puppies that no one else would take.

Through them and Rose, (one of the puppies that looked at me once and it was all over) and with another woman, our Pit Bull rescue was born. Having worked in the animal/rescue field for almost twenty years, I felt equipped to take on a municipal shelter job at MHRHS in Menands, NY that was offered to me.

The first day, ninety cats and kittens and twenty-five dogs were surrendered. The shelter handled twelve municipalities for Animal Control as well as individual surrenders. We handled 14,000 animals a year.

I went home the first night feeling "how could I ever make a difference with those numbers?" I thought I had experience. I realized that day that I had just touched the tip of the iceberg with ALL my experience.

So I proposed to make a difference! I became the shelter manager and immediately changed the "two week limit" on the lives of the animals in our care. Policy was, if not adopted in two weeks, they were euthanized. No exceptions. I changed that and started building a network of fosters for the tiny babies and elderly and the dogs that didn't kennel well. The young and infirm didn't fare well in stressful environments.

We changed the adoption applications to make better matches and therefore less returns. Worked on a staff that was caring, realistic, hardworking, and willing to work together, willing to learn, and showed up.

It's a stressful environment and one of the highest turnovers in all jobs. Emotions run high.

I encouraged staff to let me know if they had questions, concerns, complaints. Rotated people involved in euthanasia, as well as made it compassionate and peaceful for the animals when those choices had to be made.

The focus was on the animals. We worked closely with rescues that upheld the values of adoption we envisioned. The mind-set of "any home is better than no home" is NOT to the benefit of the animals. It's about the right match and less returns.

Education in schools with therapy dogs, available low cost spay/neuter, foster homes, working with rescues to avoid euthanasia for space, training classes, and availability after hours for questions about newly adopted animals, all enabled us to reduce the numbers of returns, therefore, reducing the numbers of homeless and unwanted animals facing euthanasia.

The thing that kept (and continues to now) me moving forward every day was/is focusing on what we accomplished, not looking at the situation as hopeless. Looking at the lives we saved and continuing to work together to save more and make sure no life was lost in vain, along with praying for direction, has served me well for over forty years in this world of sheltering and rescue.

I'm grateful to be able to speak for those that cannot and look forward to less and less homeless animals through spay/neuter, education, and working together, egoless, on behalf of the animals.

Cydney Cross, New York
Cofounder and President, Out of the Pits

Witnessing

Even during the first decade of the twentieth century, there were people with an awareness that the animals awaiting death at slaughterhouses had value beyond being someone's dinner. In his book, *The Jungle* (1906), Upton Sinclair muses, "Each one of these hogs was a separate creature. And each of them had an individuality of his own, a will of his own, a hope and a heart's desire; each was full of self-confidence, of self-importance, and a dense of dignity" (p. 40). The shame and tragedy is that over a hundred years after Sinclair wrote his exposé of the slaughterhouses of Chicago, the animals continue to suffer. Those that come face-to-face with the brutality inherent on factory farms and at slaughterhouses, the undercover investigators, and those who edit their video footage often suffer their own kind of pain.

> *I'm a former undercover investigator and currently the Investigations Manager for Compassion Over Killing. Working undercover takes a large toll on someone. It's very physically demanding and exhausting work, and there's no time for anything but the job. One of my hog farm investigations was a twelve-day on, two-day off rotation of twelve-plus hour days on-site, plus a few hours of work to do at night—reliving the horrors of the day. It's very emotionally draining and mentally exhausting work as well. You're not only witnessing the worst animal abuses you can imagine, you also need to take part in standard practices. Basically, the job duties that go along with the position you're working. This is the biggest internal conflict for any investigator—it's the hardest part of the job, and it stays with you for years to come.*
>
> *Working undercover can sometimes feel like the walls are closing in on you, and it can definitely feel like way too much to handle at times. The time I've spent in the field was one of the hardest and worst times of my life, but at*

the same time, it was also one of the best times of my life. Because as difficult as it is to perform those job duties, investigators know that if they weren't there doing it, someone else would be—and that someone would not have a camera on them to show the world what's really happening. Two of our recent investigations, Quality Pork Processors and Tyson Foods, have both gone viral upon release, reaching so many millions of people. We then get flooded with messages saying that someone has gone vegetarian or vegan after seeing our investigations. THAT is what makes it all worth it.

I've become desensitized to the footage. It's hard to avoid that after working in the field for several years because once you see it in person, watching it on a screen pales in comparison. But the release of an investigation brings all of the emotions flooding back, and that will never get old. Knowing that at that moment countless people are seeing it for the first time and making the decision to stop eating animals—that's heartwarming and overwhelming, and I can't help but get teary and choked up. So if there are any readers out there who want to get involved with helping animals but question whether they can handle it—this is what I can say. Yes, there might be compassion fatigue. Yes, there will be physical fatigue. Yes, you will cry. But nothing compares to the fulfillment you feel from knowing that you are making a difference and leading the life that you know you should.

Mike Wolf
Investigations Manager, Compassion Over Killing

• • •

I have to take a lot of breaks.

In the normal course of a day, I can work at my desk for ten to twelve hours at a time—developing campaign *strategies, drafting press releases, and recruiting new advocates. But editing undercover video footage from animal breeding facilities and slaughterhouses is a completely different type of work.*

The projects are daunting. My job is to screen hundreds of hours of video captured by undercover investigators working for national animal protection organizations. I spend hours, days, and often weeks compiling the most impactful and disturbing clips captured during investigations. I often face the "problem" of having too much graphic footage to fit into a reasonable video length the average viewer could endure. I often have to decide between which brutal scenes best conveys the message. It's never an easy decision.

One of the biggest challenges is striking a balance. How do I select scenes that are graphic enough to convey the reality of what animals are forced to endure without making it so graphic that people refuse to watch it or turn it off in horror within a few seconds.

Reviewing footage is always hardest at first. I eventually establish a disconcerting rhythm, where I become almost numb to the abuses on the screen. But I will <u>never</u> get used to the sounds.

The blood-curdling scream of a mother pig with her head stuck under a thick metal bar of a holding cage will always haunt me. The screaming and shrieking of injured and dying animals is never silenced. I have broken down crying, become physically ill—but I don't know if someone who didn't have this visceral reaction would be able to truly tell the story.

One of the saddest parts is knowing that by the time the footage makes its way from the undercover investigator to me, all of the animals in the footage are already dead. There will be no reprieve. Watching footage taken over the course of months, I get to know and recognize some of the animals in the breeding facilities. I name them—partially to keep track of them (easier than memorizing their six digit numbers) but also because I think they deserve a name. I eventually watch them all die or be shipped off to be killed. But I believe there is honor in their story being shared and that they didn't die in vain.

 I want viewers to see animals as individuals—as the unique, distinct beings they are. It's easier for most to think of individual pigs as a faceless mass where pork, bacon, and sausage are born. But that gets harder once a pig has a name. I need people to see "Penny" because the investigators, video editors, and advocates are Penny's last chance of being heard.

Elizabeth Putsche, Baltimore, Maryland
Founder & Executive Director, Photographers for Animals

7
Wounded Warriors

Once you fully apprehend the vacuity of a life without struggle, you are equipped with the basic means of salvation.

—Tennessee Williams

WHETHER YOU'RE AN ethical vegan, animal advocate, or both, the preceding stories demonstrate the powerful emotions that can be triggered by your values and your actions. So what's to be done about all these emotional responses that keep arising? First and foremost, we must accept that our feelings are normal reactions to the cruelty and injustices we witness in the world and not try to deny them. Even if we do try to push our emotions aside or bury them deep inside, they always have a way of making their presence known, usually by expressing themselves somatically; headaches, stomach aches, and physical exhaustion can, at times, all be indicators of unexpressed emotions. Once we've acknowledged the validity and source of our feelings, and the more aware we are of what our bodies are trying to tell us, the more primed we'll be to take effective action. Then we have two choices: we can turn the emotions against ourselves and others, or we can choose ways to express those emotions through actions that are healthier and more productive.

Connecting physical distress to our emotions begins by noticing how our bodies respond when, for example, we're angry, sad, frustrated, or nervous. For example, does your face feel hot and flushed when you're pissed off? When you hear doleful news, do you always get a lump in your throat? If you're frustrated, do you clench your jaw? And what happens when you're anxious? Perhaps your stomach feels queasy or your palms get sweaty? Paying attention to the information provided by your body when you're emotionally triggered by a situation can prepare you for managing those feelings and impulses.

Once you've become familiar with your body's particular warning system, the next time you notice one of its physiological signs, try these calming breathing techniques to temporarily dissipate the strong feelings and/or powerful impulses. Find a place where you can sit quietly, where there will be no distractions. Close your eyes, and breathe in slowly through your nose and then slowly out through pursed lips. Begin by breathing in slowly for a count of two and out slowly for a count of two. Do that twice. Then breathe in slowly for a count of three and out slowly for a count of three. Do this three times. Finally, breathe in slowly for a count of four and out for a count of four. Try doing this for five minutes at which time you'll probably notice yourself feeling calmer. Initially, you may find it difficult to breathe in and/or out for more than two or three counts. That's fine. Start with what feels doable, and slowly work your way up to four. The goal of this exercise is to relax you, not make you more anxious by having to struggle with your breathing. Or try this one. Once you're in your quiet place, begin to breathe in slowly through your nose and then exhale slowly through pursed lips. Once you've got the rhythm down, when you take your next inhale, imagine the breath slowly moving to the top of your head. Then on the exhale, imagine the breath slowly moving down toward your feet. Again, try to work up to holding both the inhale and the exhale for a count of four. Continue this pattern until calmness envelops you (Brown & Gerbarg, 2012). And here's a third option. Breathe in through your nose for four counts, hold for seven counts, and then breathe out through pursed lips for eight counts. As with the other breathing techniques, initially you may not be able to control the breaths for the prescribed counts, so only do what feels manageable. Remember to be patient with yourself; if you've never done breathing exercises before, the process might feel a little strange at first. But once you become comfortable breathing in this manner, you'll likely see results pretty quickly. There are so many wonderful breathing techniques you can avail yourself of, and I encourage you to find the ones that work best for you. If, however, you find yourself constantly struggling to do the breath work, it's best to stop and check with a doctor to make sure these exercises are not contraindicated for you.

Shifting your focus away from your distressing and overwhelming thoughts to an activity that is mentally absorbing can also help settle you down. Did you ever notice that in any given moment you can multitask like mad or have dozens of thoughts scurrying around your brain, but when you need to concentrate on getting something important done, your brain can only focus on that one task? That's quite normal. So find an activity that is mentally engaging enough to hold your attention, something where your mind isn't likely to wander. For example, this could be a challenging work or school project, strenuous exercise, or speaking to a friend who needs your advice. You may not yet know what kind of activities will accomplish this goal for you, so the next time you find yourself fully absorbed in a task, make a note of that activity. Eventually, you'll have compiled a go-to list of options, which you can readily use. This change in focus also puts the brakes on rumination. When we ruminate about horrors we've seen or heard about, it's like playing a disturbing video over and over. The first time we watch it, it's likely we'll find our bodies exhibiting stress responses, such as a queasy stomach, tense muscles, unsettled breathing, or we may begin zoning out. And if we continue viewing the same harrowing images, we're keeping our bodies in this uncomfortable place. We need to give our minds and bodies a chance to calm down. By bringing our attention to something absorbing but not disquieting, we're giving ourselves a bit of much-needed relief.

Here's another option to temporarily quell your anxiety. Find a quiet place to sit, and then settle in on a chair or couch. Lean back and plant your feet on the floor (you may use a pillow if your feet don't reach). Close your eyes and place one of your hands on your chest and the other on your upper belly. Focus and keep your attention on the movement of your breath: the inhales and exhales, the rising and falling of your chest and belly. Breathe slowly and calmly. Continue till you feel relief.

A little imagery exercise can also help move you from high anxiety to a calmer state. Find a comfortable place to sit—a place where you won't be interrupted—and close your eyes. Take five deep and slow breaths. After the fifth breath, you should notice a diminishment of tension in your body. You are now ready to begin imagining a place where you would like to be at that moment. It can be a place that really exists or one that you create with your imagination. Wherever the place is, just make sure it's a happy and calm space for you. The details of the location are very important, so make sure you allot enough time to do this exercise completely. Is the place inside or outside? What surrounds you? Trees? An ocean? A fireplace? Is anyone with you? If so, is it a person or animal that is currently in your life or someone imaginary? What does the place smell like? Pine trees? Fresh-baked pie? The cologne of someone you love? What sounds do you notice? Falling rain? A crackling fire? Music playing in the distance? What's the feeling you get while in this special place? Do you feel elated? Peaceful? Safe? The more specific you can be, the better the result will be. Once you can really experience your special place, stay there until you notice yourself calming down. Now you'll always have a place to escape to (and one that is free!) whenever you need a brief "vacation."

And never underestimate the healing power of being around people who truly understand you and are able to validate your feelings. So do cultivate a strong support network. Having people you can vent to, or just spend time with, can be very restorative.

Finally, a really useful and productive way to channel feelings of outrage and sadness over animal abuse is to come up with a strategy to devote more time to helping animals. Channeling our anger, sadness, and frustration in this way is extremely empowering. And it doesn't matter if the plan is on a small or large scale; all that matters is that the plan exists at all. Whether you decide that your vocation will be helping animals by becoming a veterinarian, vet tech, marine biologist, primatologist, or head of an animal organization or that helping them will be your avocation through volunteer advocacy work, the goal is the same—to improve the lives of animals. You now have a healthy outlet for all the feelings you've been carrying inside.

> *In the '60s, I was a vegan child raised as a carnivore. Our family often gave forever homes to stray cats. Meat from my dinner plate was often discreetly fed to our companion animals, camouflaged with A-1 Sauce or flushed down the toilet. Growing up loving four-legged furry friends led to early confusion and sadness...why was I loving some and eating others? My heart connection to animals was forever wide open. In the '80s, Boston University offered The Vegetarian Dining Hall and my road to veganism commenced. Years passed and my angst about the enormity of others eating animals was unbearable. As animal rights became a part of my life, I heard sayings like "Don't mourn, organize" and "Light a candle, don't curse the darkness." So in 1993, I created Healthy Gourmet To-Go, a vegan meal delivery business to help busy people eat fewer animals. Twenty-four years*

later, HGTG continues feeding people plus opening hearts and minds to animal suffering. Making a difference in this way is how I get through the day.
Roni Shapiro, Woodstock, New York

I do want to emphasize again that one's feelings should never be squashed or minimized. The aforementioned strategies are useful when you either need to calm yourself down immediately or want to refocus your energy in ways that help both you and animals. These techniques help assuage feelings that are temporary and not completely overpowering. They are not meant to replace the processing of your feelings and uncovering and understanding the reasons for your distressed state. If, however, you notice that whenever you're confronted with images or news of animal abuse/neglect you have intense physical and emotional reactions which catapult you into a depressed and/or anxious state which you're not able to "shake"; you find that the decisions you've been making and/or actions you've been taking are harmful or inappropriate but feel beyond your control; or you realize you have been feeling disconnected from life for a while with no discernible cause, it might be an indication that some other experiences in your life, past or present, are also at play. It's also conceivable that the reason for your change in mood, outlook, and/or disposition is that you have been traumatized by something you've witnessed or experienced, and you might be suffering from Post-Traumatic Stress Disorder (PTSD). "Depression and anxiety often have traumatic antecedents, as does mental illness" (Levine, 1997, p. 45).

Belleruth Naparstek, in her book, *Invisible heroes: Survivors of trauma and how they heal* (2004), says people with PTSD "oscillate between very intense feelings and their opposite: numbness and internal deadness" (p. 106). Moreover, she adds, "Trauma sets in motion a biochemical chain of events that can result in chronic pain and an unusual number of medical problems" (p. 68). Gastrointestinal issues, extreme fatigue, skin issues, hair loss, and cystitis are just some of the physical manifestations of trauma she speaks about. However, before assuming that your physical or mental maladies are the result of a traumatic event or history, do consult with your doctor first to rule out any medical causes.

You may be wondering if trauma affects only certain types of people or arises only under specific conditions. The answer is no; trauma can touch all kinds of people and can be the result of quite diverse experiences. "Common occurrences can produce traumatic aftereffects that are just as debilitating as those experienced by veterans of combat or survivors of childhood abuse" (Levine, 1997, p. 45). So while there is no specific situation guaranteed to induce trauma nor is there one type of person destined to develop PTSD after experiencing or witnessing something horrible, there are a few indicators that trauma could potentially be the outcome of a particular event. They include witnessing intense violence, being physically close to or participating in the event, perceiving the situation as intolerable, having prolonged exposure to unbearable conditions, possessing limited resiliency, and having the surrounding culture sanction the event, thus depriving the person of vital social support within their community. However, timely and appropriate emotional aid following a traumatizing event can militate against someone developing PTSD.

Based on the above description, any one of us might be susceptible to trauma's effects, especially those individuals who put themselves in harm's way to aid and protect animals or care for the ones that have already been harmed physically or emotionally. I'm speaking of the people on the front lines, those who consistently witness or pick up the pieces from those who have engaged in abuse and neglect. "Traumatic events...undermine the belief systems that give meaning to human experience," (Herman, 1992, p. 51). We often hear people say that they can't wrap their heads around the evil that people do, that it's impossible to bear. But then, is running away or shutting down our only recourse? Of course not. But sometimes, in the moment, that's all we're able to do, consciously or unconsciously. "We have learned that trauma is not just an event that took place sometime in the past; it is also the imprint left by that experience on mind, brain, and body" (Van der Kolk, 2015, p. 21).

While some people experience PTSD as an amalgam of physical symptoms, for others, the problem has more to do with feeling cut off from the life they used to live. "People flee the scene *psychically*, by becoming distant, detached, and emotionally disconnected from the realities on the ground" (Naparstek, 2004, p. 76).

But remember—not every overwhelming, frightening, or disturbing experience is destined to lead to traumatic symptoms. For many people, being exposed to something horrific may occupy their thoughts for a short time before eventually fading in intensity. Two people can witness or be part of a very disturbing event, but only one of them will develop PTSD. We all process information differently and vary in our capacities for viewing and enduring disturbing incidents. If you have any suspicion that you might be suffering from PTSD, seeking the counsel of a therapist trained in trauma therapy is highly recommended. Therapies that use a mind-body approach have been found to be very effective for many people. These include Somatic Experiencing, Eye Movement Desensitization and Reprocessing (EMDR), Sensorimotor Psychotherapy, and Guided Imagery. However, there are plenty of other treatment options from which to choose, so do your research to find one that meets your needs.

Conclusion

THE LIFE STORIES shared by the people in this book evince that the world is filled with compassionate, bright, strong, tenacious, and immensely courageous human beings. These are the people the world's animals depend upon for their very lives. While that may seem like a huge burden to some, it's a challenge willingly and happily taken on by the countless individuals who devote their lives to animals. And I have no doubt that the qualities and experiences of these people are shared by many of you.

There are times, however, when the reality of animal suffering envelops us like a noxious cloud, bringing up powerful and distressing feelings along the way. It's during these moments that we need to pause and then use strategies that can help us dissipate this pall. This book offered some techniques to make that happen, and hopefully, they will prove useful to some of you. There will be times, however, when these methods will be insufficient to subdue those powerful thoughts and feelings. Consequently, over time, you might find they become your constant companion; these are assuredly not the type of associates you need in your life. If that happens, seeking professional counsel is strongly recommended. While I've listed a few therapeutic options in this book that are known to have helped many people dealing with a traumatic past or present, these suggestions do not by any means represent an exhaustive list. I encourage anyone who might require the assistance of a therapist to do your own research so you can find both a technique and a clinician that feels right for you.

Finally, as you reflect on the stories that these brave and dedicated people have shared, know that you're not alone in your struggles nor in your successes. You're part of a growing community of passionate people all working for the same goal—to make life better for the animals.

References

Brown, R. P., & Gerbarg, P. L. (2012). *The healing power of the breath.* Boston, MA: Shambhala Publications.

Herman, J. (1992). *Trauma & recovery.* New York: Basic Books.

Kahler, S. (2015, January 17). Moral stress the top trigger in veterinarians' compassion fatigue. *Journal of the American Veterinary Medical Association.* Retrieved from https://www.avma.org/News/JAVMANews/Pages/150101e.aspx

Krystal, B. (2016, May 16). The next frontier for vegan restaurants? Not calling yourself a vegan restaurant. *The Washington Post.* Retrieved from https://www.washingtonpost.com/news/going-out-guide/

Levine, P. (1997). *Waking the tiger.* Berkeley, CA: North Atlantic Books.

Naparstek, B. (2004). *Invisible heroes: Survivors of trauma & how they heal.* New York: Bantum Dell Books.

Sinclair, U. (1906). *The jungle*. New York: Doubleday.

Van der Kolk, B. (2015). *The body keeps the score*. New York: Penguin Books.

Printed in Great Britain
by Amazon